SERIES EDITORS

TRACY L. PELLETT   JACK RUTHERFORD   CLAUDIA BLACKMAN

Skills, Drills & Strategies for
Racquetball

David Walker

Holcomb Hathaway, Publishers
Scottsdale, Arizona 85250

Copyright © 1999 by Holcomb Hathaway, Inc.

 Holcomb Hathaway, Publishers, Inc.
6207 North Cattle Track Road
Scottsdale, Arizona 85250

10 9 8 7 6 5 4 3 2 1

ISBN 1-890871-17-6

All rights reserved. No part of this book may be
reproduced, in any form or by any means,
without permission in writing from the publisher.

Printed in the United States of America.

Contents

About the Author   vi
Preface   vii

SECTION 1   Preliminaries   1

HISTORY   1
NATIONAL ORGANIZATIONS   2
CONDITIONING   3
    General Conditioning   3
    Specific Conditioning   6
    Safety Notes   6
WARM-UP   7
EQUIPMENT   9
    Footwear   9
    Clothing   9
    Protective Eyewear   9
    Rackets   9
    Accessories   12

SECTION 2   The Game   13

THE GAME   13
    Physical Skills   13
    Participants   14
    Game Action   14

RULES 14
    Serving 14
    Return of Serve and Rally 15
    Hinders 16
COURT 16
SCORING 17
ETIQUETTE 17

SECTION 3 Skills and Drills 19

SKILL 1   BASIC STROKES   19
    Grip 19
    Wrist Action 24
    Ready Position 24
    Forehand Stroke 25
    Backhand Stroke 30
    Overhead Stroke 36

SKILL 2   BASIC OFFENSIVE SHOTS   41
    Passing Shots 41
    Kill Shots 46

SKILL 3   BASIC DEFENSIVE SHOTS   53
    Ceiling Shots 54
    Around-the-Wall Ball 55

SKILL 4   PLAYING OFF THE BACK WALL   59
    Back Wall Rebound on the Fly 60
    Back Wall Rebound from a Corner 61
    Desperation Back Wall Shots (Hitting into the back wall) 67

SKILL 5   SERVE AND RETURN OF SERVE   70
    Drive Serve 71
    Lob Serve 74
    Half-Lob Serve 75
    Z Serve 76
    High Z Serve 77
    Return of Serve 79
    Dealing with Problems on Specific Serves 80
    Return of Serve/Serve Drill for Two Players 81

SKILL 6   ADVANCED OFFENSIVE SHOTS   81
    Drop Shot and Soft Corner Kill   81
    Splat Shot   82
    Overhead Kill Shot   82
SKILL 7   ADVANCED DEFENSIVE SHOTS   84
    High Z or Three-Wall Shot   84

SECTION 4   Strategies   87

PSYCHOLOGICAL STRATEGIES FOR
PERFORMANCE ENHANCEMENT   87
    Concentration   87
    Visualization   88
    Stress Management/Relaxation   88
GAME STRATEGIES   90
    Center Court Position   90
    Offense   90
    Defense   92
    Alignments   93
    Anticipating Opponent's Strategies   95
    Adjusting to Characteristics of Your Opponent   96
    Learning by Watching   97

SECTION 5   Glossary   99

Index   *103*

About the Author

David Walker has a solid foundation in racquetball, having taught beginning and advanced collegiate racquetball classes for the past fifteen years at Ricks College. He has spent thousands of hours on the courts with students, and has incorporated these teaching and observational experiences into words and pictures for those who read and use this text.

David has a broad background in many sports and activities. He competed in college and professional football and track and field, and has been very successful coaching both sports on the collegiate level. His Ricks College teaching responsibilities have included racquetball, tennis, golf, bowling, weight training, basketball, swimming, aerobics, and fitness classes. Of these, his first love has been racquetball. David received his M.Ed. from Brigham Young University, and he did his master's thesis on racquetball skill testing, establishing evaluation techniques and mastery levels for progression from beginning to advanced racquetball classes.

David is married to the former Claudia Sorensen, and they are the parents of five children: Misty, Jaclyn, Jill, Jennifer, and Kevin. They reside in Rexburg, Idaho, where David is a member of the Ricks College Physical Education faculty.

Preface

WELCOME TO THE TEACH, COACH, PLAY SERIES

The books in the *Teach, Coach, Play* series emphasize a systematic learning approach to sports and activities. Both visual and verbal information are presented so that you can easily understand the material and improve your performance.

Built-in learning aids help you master each skill in a step-by-step manner. Using the cues, summaries, skills, drills, and illustrations will help you build a solid foundation for safe and effective participation now and in the future.

This text is designed to illustrate correct techniques and demonstrate how to achieve optimal results. Take a few minutes to become familiar with the textbook's organization and features. Knowing what to expect and where to look for material will help you get the most our of the textbook, your practice time, and this course.

TO THE INSTRUCTOR

Your needs are changing, your courses are changing, your students are changing, and the demands from your administration are changing. By setting out to create a series of books that addresses many of these changes, we've created a series that:

- Provides complete, consistent coverage of each sport—the basics through skills and drills to game strategies so you can meet the needs of majors and non-majors alike.
- Includes teaching materials so that new and recently assigned instructors have the resources they need to teach the course.
- Allows you to cover exactly the sports and activities you want with the depth of coverage you want.

What's in the *Teach, Coach, Play* Series?

- Nine Activities:
    - Skills, Drills, & Strategies for Badminton
    - Skills, Drills, & Strategies for Basketball
    - Skills, Drills, & Strategies for Bowling
    - Skills, Drills, & Strategies for Golf

Skills, Drills, & Strategies for Racquetball
Skills, Drills, & Strategies for Strength Training
Skills, Drills, & Strategies for Swimming
Skills, Drills, & Strategies for Tennis
Skills, Drills, & Strategies for Volleyball
- Accompanying instructor's manuals

What's in the Student *Teach, Coach, Play* Textbooks?

The basic approach in all of the *Teach, Coach, Play* activity titles is to help students improve their skills and performance by building mastery from simple to complex levels.

The basic organization in each textbook is as follows:

Section 1 overviews history, organizations and publications, conditioning activities, safety, warm up suggestions, and equipment.

Section 2 covers exercises or skills, participants, action involved, rules, facility or field, scoring, and etiquette.

Section 3 focuses on skills and drills or program design.

Section 4 addresses a broad range of strategies specifically designed to improve performance now and in the future.

Section 5 provides a convenient glossary of terms.

Supplements to Support You and Your Students

The *Teach, Coach, Play* books provide useful and practical instructional tools. Each activity is supported by its own manual. Each of these instructor's manuals includes classroom management notes, safety guidelines, teaching tips, ideas for inclusion of students with special needs, drills, lesson plans, evaluation notes, test bank, and a list of resources for you.

Preliminaries

SECTION 1

Congratulations on your decision to learn about and participate in the game of racquetball. Racquetball offers a unique combination to the sports and fitness community: (1) a game where basic knowledge and adequate skills can be taught and learned in a short period of time; (2) a fitness workout where excellent aerobic exercise can accompany participation in a vigorous game; and (3) a sport where quality competition is available to players matched by skill levels, from beginners to professionals.

HISTORY

Racquetball began in the United States in 1949 when Joe Sobek, a tennis pro from Bridgeport, Connecticut, decided to develop a racket game to play on a handball court. Paddleball was played at that time using flat wooden paddles, but it lacked speed and accuracy, and Sobek wanted to improve on the existing game. He was first to incorporate stringed rackets into the new game, which he called "paddle rackets." After trying many existing types of balls, he also developed the first ball made specifically for paddle rackets. Sobek organized a set of rules adapted from handball to go along with his new rackets and balls, and the game of racquetball evolved from there. Because of his innovations Sobek is generally recognized as the founder of racquetball as we know it today.

The game spread across the country during the next two decades and began to be incorporated into YMCAs and recreation department programs. The names "paddle tennis" and "paddleball" were also used until 1969, when the International Racquetball Association (IRA) was formed as the official governing body of the sport. At its first organizational meeting the association adopted the name "racquetball" and recognized it as a worldwide sport. The IRA has been replaced in this country by the United States Racquetball Association **(USRA),** formerly the AARA, headquartered in Colorado Springs, Colorado. More specific information on the AARA is available later in this chapter.

USRA

During the late 1960s and 1970s, "Dr. Bud" Meuhleisen and Charles Brumfield were the first dominant players who helped bring recognition to the sport with their style of finesse and strategy. Dr. Bud also gave clinics across the nation to promote the spread of racquetball. These early players were followed by Marty

Hogan who brought the term "power racquetball" to the game. Marty won many championships by overpowering his opponents with his booming shots. Today there are many superb racquetball players competing on local, regional, state, and national levels who are bringing popularity to the game they love.

Racquetball has experienced phenomenal growth and popularity in recent years and is enjoyed worldwide by millions of participants of all ages and both sexes. Participants have more discretionary leisure and fitness time than ever before. The popularity of racquetball has influenced schools, community centers, private enterprises, and others to include racquetball court space in their facilities, and court space is becoming more accessible as these providers attempt to meet the increasing demand. Rackets and eyewear are made of space-age materials, and equipment is readily available and very affordable. Even the fashion world is involved, influencing court attire and footwear.

Racquetball has become a universal fitness and recreational activity. Most college curriculums now include racquetball, and it continues to grow in popularity and participation because it offers recreation, competition, fitness benefits, and a great deal of fun. Racquetball has a great future heading into the next century and is currently being considered as a sport in the Olympic Games.

NATIONAL ORGANIZATIONS

The United States Racquetball Association (USRA), formerly the American Amateur Racquetball Association (AARA), is the only recognized governing body for the sport of racquetball in the United States and is a member of the International Racquetball Federation. The USRA sponsors local, regional, and national competitions and provides insurance and other benefits to registered members. For more information on the USRA, contact them at this address:

United States Racquetball Association (USRA)

United States Racquetball Association (USRA)
1685 West Uintah
Colorado Springs, CO 80904-2921
Phone: (719) 635-5396
Fax: (719) 635-0685

The American Collegiate Racquetball Association (ACRA) has been the governing body over intercollegiate racquetball in the United States and has operated under the umbrella of the USRA. Currently, the USRA has taken over the supervision of the intercollegiate games and assigned regional representatives around the country. Many collegiate competitions are sponsored by colleges and universities throughout the school year. Regional championships are held each year during February and March, and these have been followed by a national collegiate tournament. For more information on intercollegiate racquetball competition, contact the USRA at the address above.

Many local groups sponsor area competitions. For more information on local tournaments, contact a local racket club professional or a college racquetball club advisor in your area.

Publications and Resource Materials

There are many books about racquetball on the market today. These can be referenced at a local library and may be purchased in bookstores, racket club pro shops, sporting goods stores, and other locations where sports publications are sold.

There are three magazines dealing exclusively with the sport of racquetball:

Killshot is the only racquetball magazine that is financed by subscription dues. It is released five times per year. For information, contact *Killshot*, P.O. Box 8036, Paducah, Kentucky 42002-8036.

Racquetball Magazine is sponsored by the USRA and is released six times per year. USRA members can receive this magazine as part of their annual $20 membership fee. Subscription is only $15 per year. For information, contact *Racquetball Magazine,* 1685 West Uintah, Colorado Springs, Colorado 80904-2921.

Total Racquetball is sponsored by Ektelon and is released annually. It is an Ektelon equipment catalog but also features many great tips and other information. Ektelon will send *Total Racquetball* to you at no charge. Call 1-800-449-6834.

There are excellent racquetball training videos available for use by racquetball enthusiasts. Three are listed here:

Playing Smart is Ektelon's instructional video. It features Team Ektelon's top-ranked players and contains game strategy and tips to help improve the level of play. Send $19.95 to Ektelon, 8929 Aero Drive, San Diego, California 92123.

Learn Your Lessons and *Practice Drills* are available from the USRA. Each is $19.95, plus a $4.95 shipping and handling fee per order. Send orders to the USRA at the address listed above.

CONDITIONING

Racquetball can be a physically demanding activity. Therefore, players should choose to participate in a conditioning program prior to and in conjunction with their involvement in racquetball. Cardiovascular endurance, strength and quickness, flexibility, and body composition are all physical factors that affect participants' performance in racquetball. Each of these can be improved by employing an appropriate conditioning program.

General Conditioning

Cardiovascular endurance can be improved by participation in conditioning activities as outlined by the American College of Sports Medicine. These activities could include jogging, walking, swimming, biking, or any other exercises that include training *3 to 5 days per week* in *activities involving large muscle groups* at an *intensity level requiring 60 to 85 percent of maximal heart rate.* (Maximal heart rate is found by subtracting your age from 220. A 20-year-old college student would have a maximal heart rate of 220 – 20 = 200, with a training heart rate zone of 120 to 170 beats per minute.) The *length of each training session* is determined by the intensity of the exercises involved: lower intensity activities such as walking or stop-and-go exercises should last 45 to 60 minutes, while higher intensity activities such as running or competitive racquetball should last 20 to 30 minutes, depending on the exercise.

The *1991 ACRA/AARA Intercollegiate Racquetball Manual* states that racquetball is an excellent cardiorespiratory conditioning activity, having been shown to bring about gains in endurance due to its aerobic nature. According to the ACRA/AARA manual, a typical racquetball player will maintain a heart rate in the range of 80 to 85 percent of maximum during a competitive racquetball **match.** The **serve**-and-**rally** action in a racquetball game can be highly anaerobic in nature, and because of this, the participants must play hard and keep the game moving rapidly to achieve an aerobic workout. More information on aerobic training may be found in numerous books.

match
serve
rally

Figure 1.1
Star drill.

4 points

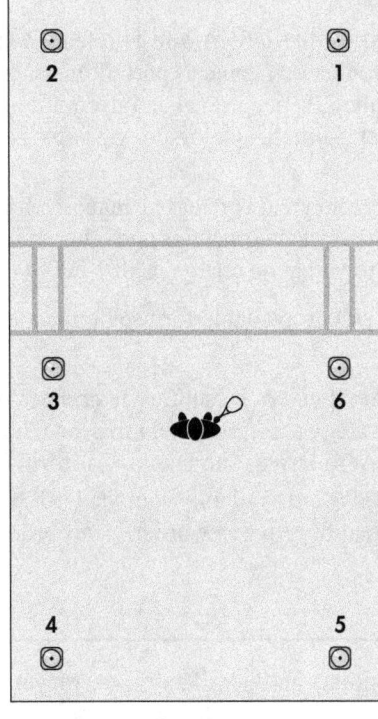
6 points

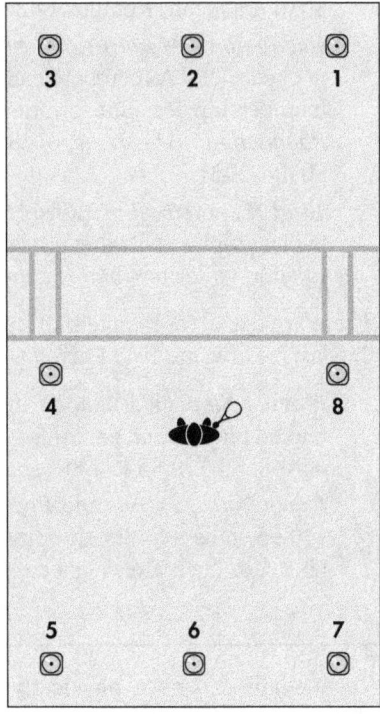
8 points

To train the anaerobic systems of the body, the intensity of the activities must be very high, and each training interval should last from 30 seconds to 2 or 3 minutes. Anaerobic training should occur on alternate days, three or four times per week. Star drills and line drills provide excellent anaerobic conditioning opportunities.

Star Drill

The objective of the star drill is to teach the participant how to move quickly to various areas of the court (to make a return shot in racquetball) and then return to the **center court** position after each shot.

1. Mark the court, or some other open area, using cones or other viable objects to designate a center spot and four, six, or eight points to the "star" (see figure 1.1). Assign a number to each point in sequence.
2. Have the participant begin on the center point in a good racquetball stance.
3. Time the drill for 15, 30, 45, or 60 seconds.
4. Determine the sequence in which the points of the star are to be touched, or designate a "caller" to call out the number of the next point to be touched after the participant has reset on the center point. (The subject should return to the center spot after touching each point and reset in a good racquetball stance.)
5. Have the participant start at the command "go," or have the caller shout out a number. The subject should quickly move to the designated point and return to the center spot, repeating this sequence until the time has expired.
6. For a score on the drill, count the number of points touched during the time allotted.

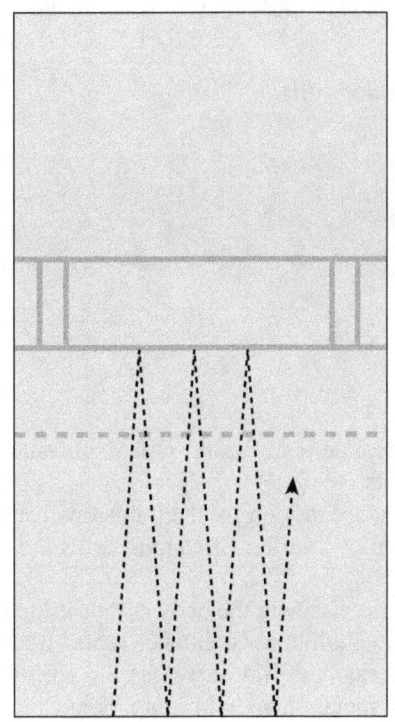
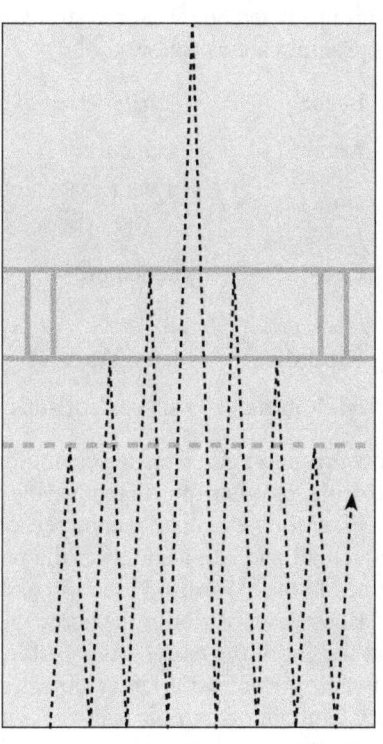

Repeat line   Progressive line touch

Figure 1.2
Line drill.

Star drills may be performed in many different ways, but the general procedure for the drills is similar. The star drills simulate racquetball game action while developing the anaerobic capabilities of the body.

Line Drill

Line drills are also referred to as shuttle runs. Two options are repeatedly touching the same line throughout the drill, or progressive line touching.

For repeat line drills, complete the following steps:

1. Start at the court **back wall,** or designated starting line, and identify a single touching line as the drill area (see figure 1.2).
2. At the command, have the participant run to the touching line and return to the starting line, repeating this procedure for the duration of the drill.

For progressive line touching, complete the following steps:

1. Begin at the court back wall or designated starting line in an open area (see figure 1.2).
2. In an open area, designate the pattern of line touching to be followed by the participant.
3. In a court, at the command, have the participant run to the **short line** and return to the back wall, to the **service line** and return to the back wall, then to the front wall and return to the back wall.
4. Repeat for the duration of the drill.

Strength and quickness are major factors for participation in racquetball. They can be improved through a program of weight training, footwork, and agility drills. Strength training should consist of a total body workout with emphasis on the mus-

line drills

back wall

short line
service line

cle groups listed below. Some strength training exercises that should be included in this program are as follows:

Legs:	squats or leg extensions/leg curls
Arms:	arm curls
	triceps extensions
	wrist curls/wrist extensions
Chest:	bench press
	flies
Shoulders:	lateral raises
Abdominals:	sit-ups/curl-ups

Footwork and agility exercises could include a series of jump rope drills, star or line drills, or other foot-maneuvering activities.

Flexibility exercises can increase the range of motion for the joints involved in racquetball and can also aid in the prevention of injuries. Stretching drills are explained in the "Warm-up" section of this book.

Body composition is the percentage of fatty tissue in the body compared to the total weight of the body. It is a factor in racquetball because it takes more strength and energy to move a larger object, and excess body fat decreases the ability to react. Combining aerobic exercise with basic metabolism to burn up more calories than are taken in is the simple formula for reducing body fat. (For more specifics on reducing body fat, refer to a good weight control and fitness text.) Participation in racquetball can also assist in body fat reduction because of the high caloric expenditure required when playing a vigorous racquetball game.

Specific Conditioning

Many individual drills can be used in conjunction with specific conditioning. In this book, many skills are accompanied by drills that could be incorporated into a conditioning program. Personal needs or preferences should determine which of these drills are used for simultaneous conditioning and practice.

There are many context-specific drills for racquetball. Context-specific drills, drills whose techniques are the same as those used in the actual game, can be an excellent method of incorporating skill practice and conditioning into the same activity. The star drill is an example of a context-specific drill for racquetball. Refer back to "General Conditioning" for information about other context-specific activities related to racquetball.

Safety Notes

protective eyewear

backcourt

thong

hinder

dehydration

1. *Always* warm up properly.
2. *Always* wear **protective eyewear.**
3. *Never* look to the **backcourt** and watch a ball being hit toward the front wall. Turn your face to the front wall prior to racket/ball contact.
4. *Always* keep wrist **thong** attached in the court.
5. *Always* observe **hinder** rules and make calls to protect all players from potential injury. No point is worth winning at the cost of an injury.
6. *Always* drink plenty of fluids to avoid **dehydration** when practicing and playing racquetball.

WARM-UP

Always warm up properly before participation in any vigorous activity, including racquetball. Begin warming up with an activity such as easy jogging, jumping rope, or other light exercise that will raise the heart rate and bring about a light perspiration on the forehead without fatigue. This will help to gradually prepare the body for the demands about to be placed on it.

Follow this preparation with stretching to help prevent injuries and allow for full range of motion when beginning the activity. Stretching can be more effective if some basic guidelines are followed:

1. It is best to stretch a muscle when it is in a relaxed state, not when it is contracted and/or weight bearing.
2. Never stretch with a jerking or bobbing motion.
3. Always stretch and hold in a static state for 15 to 30 seconds to allow the muscle to relax and stretch to its maximum.
4. Stretch the muscles controlling joints that will be used in the activity.
5. Some discomfort is not unusual during proper stretching. However, pain is a sign of a possible problem. Discontinue any stretch that causes pain. For racquetball, the following stretches are suggested:

■ Shoulder #1

Stand with shoulders perpendicular to a wall and about 1 foot from the wall. Extend the wall-side arm back and up to shoulder level. Brace the hand against the wall. While keeping the shoulders perpendicular to the wall, lean the body toward the wall to stretch the shoulder muscles. Hold. Turn around and repeat with the other arm.

■ Shoulder #2

Extend the right arm up and across the body just under the chin. With the left hand, reach up and lightly pull the right elbow toward the left shoulder, keeping the right arm fully extended. Hold. Repeat with the left arm.

■ Shoulder (and triceps) #3

Place the right hand over the shoulder and between the shoulder blades. Put the chin on the chest. Reach the left hand behind the head to the right elbow and pull the right arm toward the back. Hold. Repeat with the left arm.

■ Neck

Keep the shoulders stationary and draw circles as large as possible in the air with the top of the head. Go clockwise and counterclockwise.

■ Trunk #1

From a standing position, with hands to the sides, push the right hand down the outside of the thigh as far as possible while raising the left shoulder. Keep both feet flat on the ground. Hold. Repeat on the left side.

■ Trunk #2

Sit on the floor with legs extended together. Bend the right knee up and place the right heel on the opposite side of the left knee. Cross the left elbow to the outside of the right knee and apply pressure there with the back of the left arm. Hold. Repeat with the left leg.

■ Trunk #3

From a standing position, establish a slight bend in the knees and bend forward at the waist. Roll the shoulders forward and hang both arms as far down as possible. This is not a hamstring stretch, so relax the legs. Also, relax the lower back, allowing the upper trunk to hang and stretch. Hang for at least 10–15 seconds.

■ Groin

Sit on the floor with legs extended together. Draw the heels up to the groin area and turn the soles of the feet together. Place the elbows on the inside of each knee and gradually press the knees out and down toward the floor.

■ Legs #1

Sit on the floor with legs extended together. Lean forward and reach for the toes, keeping the backs of the legs against the floor. Reach as far as possible, relax the leg muscles, and hold.

■ Legs #2

Sit on the floor with legs spread apart and extended. Lean toward the right leg and reach with the left hand for the right toes. Keep the back of the legs against the floor. Reach as far as possible, relax the leg muscles, and hold. Repeat toward the left leg.

■ Calf/Achilles

Stand, facing the wall, about 3 feet from the wall. Step back about 12 more inches with the right foot. Lean forward with both arms extended to the wall. Bend the left knee and straighten the right knee. Push the right heel to the floor and lean the hips and upper body closer to the wall. Relax the lower right leg muscles and hold. Repeat with the left leg.

■ Wrists

Stand, facing the wall, about 18 inches from the wall. With the palm down and elbow extended, reach the right hand just above head level to the wall and bend the wrist downward. Try to place the back of the hand against the wall and apply slight pressure. Relax the wrist and hold. Next, with the palm down and elbow extended, reach the right hand down about waist level to the wall and bend the wrist upward. Try to place the palm against the wall and apply slight pressure. Relax the wrist and hold). Repeat with the left wrist.

This is not a complete list of all the possible stretches that may be performed. However, these stretches do include each major muscle group involved in racquetball. Add any other stretches preferred or necessary to feel prepared for participation in a vigorous game of racquetball.

Final warm-up should take place on the court, where participants may begin by hitting easy **forehand** and **backhand** shots and progressing to more strenuous, powerful strokes. Observe proper etiquette when two or more players are warming up on the court at the same time.

forehand
backhand

EQUIPMENT

Footwear

Proper shoes are essential to safety and performance on a racquetball court. Improper fit or lack of support can lead to injuries, and lack of adequate traction or lateral support can affect the player's ability to react on the court. Racquetball court shoes are recommended for the serious player. They meet all the necessary requirements for support and traction on a racquetball court. Other athletic shoes such as basketball or tennis shoes are less desirable but acceptable substitutes. Shoes designed for running or black-soled shoes should not be worn on the racquetball court. Running shoes are designed for straight line movement with minimal lateral support and often have a raised padded heel that affects traction and balance on a racquetball court. Black-soled shoes leave unsightly markings on the court surface and should be avoided. Low-, mid-, or high-top shoes that meet the other requirements are all acceptable. The different heights provide varying levels of support for the ankle, and the user should choose according to personal preference.

Clean, soft, and absorbent athletic socks should be worn along with the correct shoes. They provide padding to reduce stress on the feet during participation in racquetball. They absorb sweat and protect the shoe from excessive moisture. The socks should be made of cotton or some other soft, absorbent fabric.

Clothing

Shirts, shorts, and socks, which constitute the uniform, should all be clean and can be of any color. Clothing should fit comfortably and be made of absorbent fabric. Players should not play without a shirt. Perspiration is absorbed by the clothing, and drops of perspiration on the floor could be hazardous, resulting in slipping and possible injuries during play.

Headbands and wristbands are optional clothing accessories, which are worn to aid in absorption of perspiration that may interfere with the hands or face during play. They should also be clean, of any color, and made of a soft, absorbent fabric.

Protective Eyewear

USRA rules require that protective eyewear be worn by all racquetball players. Responsible court facility management also requires this. Proper protective eyewear significantly reduces the possibility of serious eye injury. Balls traveling at speeds of up to 200 miles per hour and rackets driving power shots can inflict severe damage if the eyes are not properly guarded. Be wise: *Protect your eyes!*

The USRA recommends that protective lenses be made of polycarbonate with a 3-millimeter center thickness for strength. Polycarbonate is a clear impact-resistant material that can be treated to resist scratching. It is also available with an antifog coating. Frames should be padded to protect the nose and forehead. Prescription lenses made of polycarbonate can be obtained to protect those who wear glasses. Normal prescription lenses are not recommended in place of approved protection.

Fashion and design should not interfere with the protective features of safe eyewear. Approved eyewear comes in many styles and colors to provide a broad selection for the image-conscious user. For a complete list of approved racquetball eyewear, contact the USRA national office.

Rackets

Rackets come in a wide variety of sizes, shapes, frame materials, and price ranges. The more skilled a player becomes, the bigger factor the racket will be in his or her results. Before purchasing a racket, experiment with different models to determine the characteristics you prefer in your racket.

Rackets may not exceed 21 inches in length and are available in standard, midsized, and oversized heads (see figure 1.3). Many shapes and designs are available, but the most popular are the teardrop and rectangular shapes. Head sizes range from 85 to 112 square inches. Most players now use the midsized (94–98 sq. in.) or oversized (98–112 sq. in.) rackets because they allow for a larger sweet spot and more margin of error in contacting the ball.

Grip size is also important to the fit and control of the user, and grips vary in size from $3^{1}/_{16}$ to $3^{3}/_{4}$ inches. The grip, or handle, should fit comfortably in the palm of the hand with the middle and/or fourth finger touching the base of the thumb.

Early rackets had wooden frames, but today's rackets are made from space-age technology, primarily of aluminum, injection-molded composite, or compression-molded composite materials (see figure 1.3). The aluminum rackets are the most durable. However, more advanced players prefer the power and control they achieve from the composite rackets.

Composite rackets are made two ways: injection-molding with short fibers machine-injected into a mold and compression-molding with long fibers placed in a mold by hand. The compression-molded rackets offer higher response and ball control and are used by more elite players than the other types of rackets.

Rackets range in price from ten dollars to hundreds of dollars, requiring the purchaser to be knowledgeable for proper racket selection. Before making a purchase, rent or borrow different rackets to get a feel for individual preferences. Each type of racket has advantages and disadvantages, so try to determine the most desirable and appropriate one before making a purchase.

String material and string tension are two more factors to be considered. Most rackets come from the manufacturer already strung with nylon. Strings may be synthetic nylon, natural gut, graphite, plastic, metal, monofilament, or a combination of these materials. If a racket needs to be restrung because of string damage or to change tension, specify the type of string material (usually nylon) with tension at some point between 25 and 50 pounds. Lesser tension allows for greater power

Figure 1.3
Rackets.

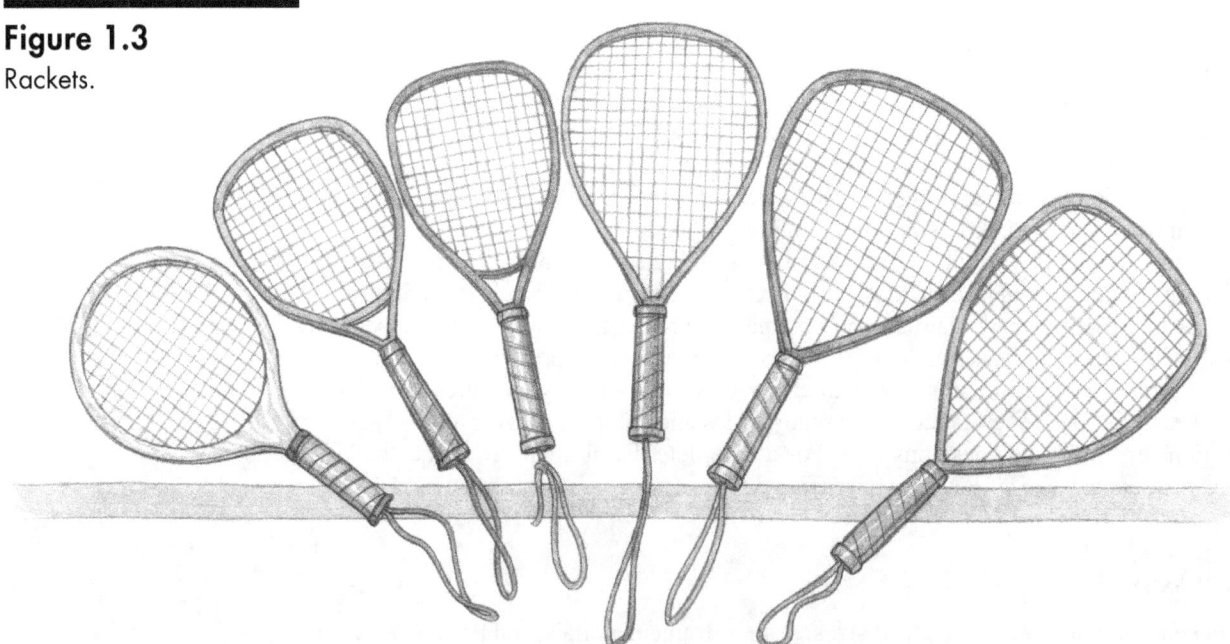

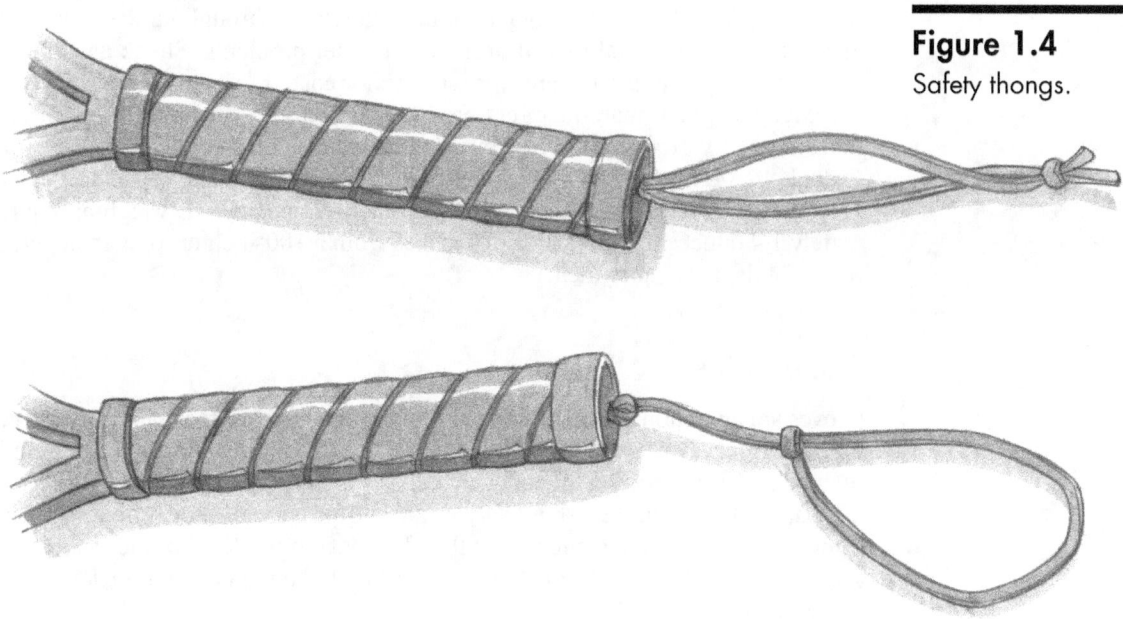

Figure 1.4
Safety thongs.

whereas higher tension produces more ball control. Most players feel comfortable with tension of around 30 pounds. Always read the instructions that come with a new racket for the manufacturer's recommendations.

All rackets should have a safety thong connected to the handle (see figure 1.4). This must be attached to the wrist at all times during play. Rackets may have a single loop, a slip loop, or even a velcro wristband. Replacement thongs are available at most sporting goods stores and racket club pro shops.

Shock absorbers, or dampeners, are a relatively new accessory that is woven between the strings at the base of the string bed (see figure 1.5). Their purpose is to reduce the string vibration passed through the racket to the hand and arm when

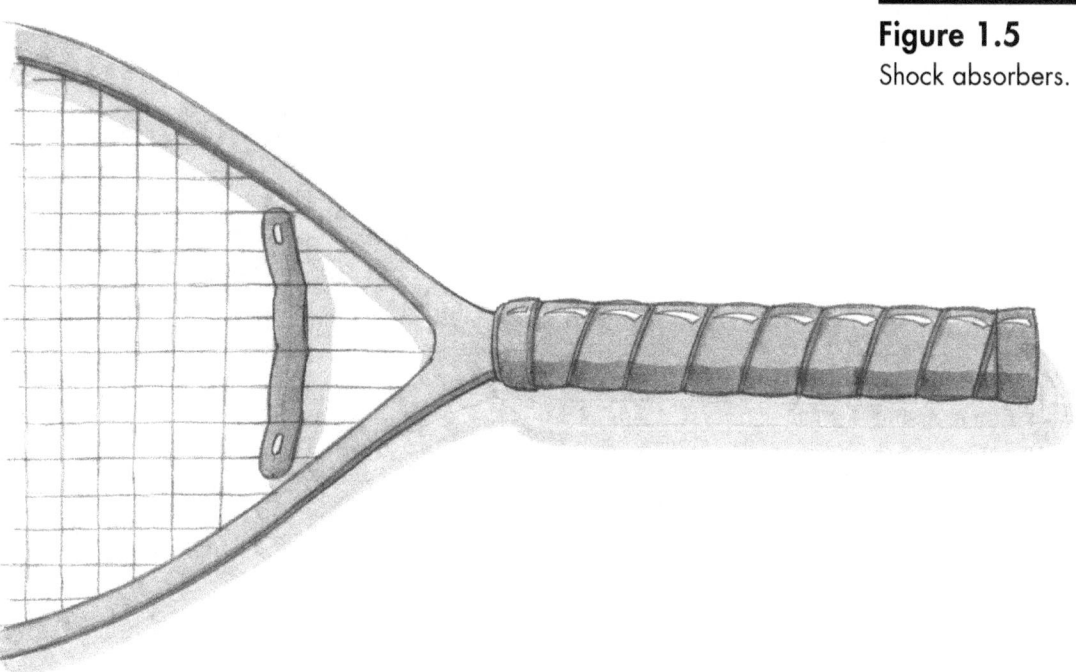

Figure 1.5
Shock absorbers.

the racket contacts the ball. They minimize vibrations throughout the racket frame and reduce the potential risk of arm and shoulder problems. Shock absorbers are becoming very popular and are worth the minor cost.

Many different manufacturers produce racquetballs. Look for the USRA endorsement to verify that the ball meets the specifications set forth by the USRA. Only USRA-approved balls may be used in an USRA-sanctioned tournament. (The official specifications require a $2^{1}/_{4}$-inch diameter ball, weighing approximately 1.4 ounces, to bounce 68–72 inches from a 100-inch drop in a temperature of 70–74 degrees Fahrenheit.)

Accessories

Gloves are an optional item but are an important accessory for many players. Players wear gloves to help prevent their racket from slipping in their hand and to maintain a firmer grip on the racket handle, especially when moisture builds up on the hand. Quality gloves should stay soft and provide a good gripping surface. They should fit the hand snugly to allow for maximum "feel" of the racket. Many styles are available, so personal preference should be the deciding factor in which glove, if any, is needed.

Racket covers are usually provided with the purchase of a good racket. They are beneficial in protecting the racket from rough treatment or accidents when not in use. Extreme temperatures can shorten the life of the strings, particularly direct sunlight or severe cold.

An equipment bag is another optional accessory that can be valuable for the avid racquetball player. It can keep all the racquetball equipment and accessories together and can carry extra rackets, balls, eyewear, and so forth that may be needed to replace damaged equipment during play.

The Game

SECTION 2

THE GAME

Racquetball has become a worldwide game played by more than ten million people. Participants include males and females, young and old, world-class and recreational athletes. The game appeals to so many because it offers an excellent cardiovascular workout in a competitive setting with minimal equipment and can include two, three, or four players. High skill is not a prerequisite to participation in an enjoyable game of racquetball. Most anyone can participate after only a few minutes of instruction. Still, those who have acquired great skill in the game also have the opportunity for high-level competition.

A brief introduction to the game of racquetball is provided in the following paragraphs. They include (1) the physical skills involved in racquetball, (2) the number of participants in a game of racquetball, and (3) a simple explanation of game action in racquetball.

Physical Skills

There are a number of physical skills involved in the game of racquetball. Each of these skills can be developed through practice and participation in a program designed to improve that particular skill. The racket skills are hand-eye coordination, forehand shot, backhand shot, change of pace (power or soft touch), and serving. The footwork skills are agility, quickness, shot setup, pivot, and stroke.

The skills of **anticipation,** shot selection, and **shot placement** are also big assets on the racquetball court. The game is played at such a high speed that good anticipation skills will give a player the advantage of not relying simply on reaction ability. Anticipating the path of the ball and its final destination as it ricochets around the court will many times allow the player to move into the proper position without chasing the ball. Proper shot selection and shot placement are essential. It is important to know what type of shots to hit from certain areas of the court and where to hit them. These decisions are also based on opponent's position, shot angles available, the players' strengths and weaknesses, and their opponents' abilities.

anticipation
shot placement

Participants

singles
cutthroat
doubles

Racquetball may be played with two (**singles**), three (**cutthroat**), or four (**doubles**) players. Singles is a one-on-one competition. Cutthroat is a rotating two-on-one game where the server plays against the other two players, and the serve is systematically rotated between the players as each server loses a rally. Doubles is one team of two members playing against another team of two members. Scoring is the same in all types of games with specific order of serve rules applying to cutthroat and doubles.

Game Action

service zone
receiver

fly
safety zone

The game of racquetball is a serve-and-rally game. Play begins with the server(s) in the **service zone** and the **receiver**(s) in the backcourt. One player or team serves to the opponent(s) by hitting the ball off a bounce directly to the front wall. The ball then rebounds and, in order to be a legal serve, must land in the backcourt area between the short line and the base of the back wall before striking two sidewalls, the back wall, or the ceiling. The receiver may hit the legally served ball on the **fly** or after one bounce off the floor, observing the **safety zone** rules. The ball must be returned before bouncing on the floor twice. The return of a serve, and any subsequent shots, may rebound off any surface in the court so long as the ball reaches the front wall on the return before hitting the floor. Players or teams alternate hitting the ball during a rally. The rally continues until one side is unable to legally keep the ball in play. Points are scored based on scoring rules for racquetball.

RULES

Serving

The order of serve is determined by a coin toss or other acceptable method. The serve then proceeds as follows:

1. The server stands on or within the boundary lines of the service box to serve.
2. The ball must be dropped and served off the first bounce and must be hit directly to the front wall.
3. The ball hitting any other court surface before contacting the front wall on the serve constitutes an **out serve.**
4. On the rebound, the ball must hit the floor behind the back edge of the short line and before striking the back wall, two sidewalls, or the ceiling. Contacting one sidewall is acceptable.

out serve

fault serve
short fault
long fault
three-wall fault
ceiling fault
foot fault
screen
drive serve
drive serve zone
drive serve fault

A **fault serve** is called when the serve hits the floor on or in front of the short line (**short fault**) or before hitting the floor, the ball hits the back wall (**long fault**), two sidewalls (**three-wall fault**), or the ceiling (**ceiling fault**). Other fault serves include the server or partner (in doubles) not starting and staying in the service zone until the serve passes the short line (**foot fault**), the ball passing so close to the server or partner that it prevents the receivers from clearly seeing the ball (**screen**), and the server hitting a **drive serve** down the same side of the court where he or she is serving while crossing into the **drive serve zone** with any part of his or her body or racket (**drive serve fault**). A fault serve requires that the server attempt a second serve. Two consecutive fault serves constitute an out serve.

As mentioned, out serves occur when the server fails to hit the ball directly to the front wall on the serve or hits two consecutive fault serves. Other out serves are delay of game, missed ball on serve attempt, fake serve attempt, served ball hitting serving team member (ball hitting floor first is a short fault; in doubles, partner is protected by service box), illegal ball contact on serve (double hit, carry, racket handle), ball hitting front wall and another surface simultaneously on serve (**crotch** serve), **out of order serve** in doubles, and safety zone violation (entering safety zone before ball passes short line). On the serve, a ball that simultaneously hits the back wall and the floor or the sidewall and the floor beyond the short line is a legal serve.

crotch
out of order serve

In doubles, the order of serve proceeds according to the following format: A1, B1, B2, A1, A2, B1, B2, A1, and so forth. When the first server in each game loses the serve, it is a **side out.** Thereafter, both players on each side shall serve in their established order until the end of that game. When both players are serving and the first player loses his or her serve, it is a **handout,** which means that the first server on a team loses the serve and the second player on that team now has the serve. When the second player loses the serve, it is a side out. Also, on each serve, the server's partner must stand erect in the service box with his or her back to the wall and both feet on the floor. Violation of this rule is called a foot fault, or a loss of serve if the partner is out of the service zone on a safety zone violation.

side out

handout

The 10-second time-out rule is important to understand whenever you are serving or receiving a serve. This rule allows either player or team on the court to take up to 10 seconds between serves after the other person or team is ready to play. The server or receiver may signal this short time-out by raising a hand over his or her head for the length of the time-out, or the receiver may turn his or her back on the server during the pause. The time-out must be signaled before the server starts the serving motion. This puts a responsibility on the server to always check on the receiver prior to calling the score and starting the serving motion. The rule is in place to allow each player up to 10 seconds to think about his or her upcoming strategy, analyze the previous play, rest for a moment, or whatever other purpose he or she may choose. It may be used before every serve, with no explanation necessary.

Return of Serve and Rally

Following a legal serve, there are rules that apply to the return of serve and subsequent rally:

1. The receiver must hit the ball before it makes contact with the floor more than once and return the ball to the front wall on the fly without the ball contacting the floor first.
2. The receiver may not enter the safety zone until the ball bounces beyond the short line or crosses the plane of the **receiving line** on the fly.
3. The court lines apply only on the serve and are not observed during the remainder of the rally.
4. On the subsequent returns in the rally, the players or teams alternate hits, and the ball must be returned as on the return of the serve.
5. During a rally after the serve, the ball may contact any combination of court surfaces other than the floor as long as the ball is legally returned to the front wall as explained above.
6. Players may not switch hands on the racket, disconnect the wrist thong, or contact the ball with any part of the body or uniform.
7. The ball may be touched only once consecutively by each side, and the ball cannot be carried on the **racket face** during a hit.
8. Players who violate these rules during a rally lose that rally.
9. If a player swings at the ball and misses during a rally, more attempts to return the ball may be made before the ball touches the floor a second time.
10. If a ball has been legally returned to the front wall and then goes into the **gallery,** play is stopped and the player hitting the ball into the gallery loses the rally.

receiving line

racket face

gallery

11. If the ball goes into the gallery off a player's racket without being returned to the front wall, the player attempting the return loses that rally.
12. If a ball breaks during a rally, the rally is replayed.
13. On any replay, a previous fault does not carry over to the reserve.

Hinders

There are two types of hinders, or interferences, that may be called during a rally: **dead-ball hinders** and **point hinders.** When a dead-ball hinder occurs, play is stopped and the rally is replayed. When a point hinder occurs, play is stopped and the player called for the hinder loses the rally.

Dead-ball hinders are usually called when the interference is unintentional and unavoidable, such as the ball hitting an opponent on a return shot going to the front wall, a court surface such as a door latch or light fixture causing an irregular bounce, which is called a **court hinder,** body contact between players, a screen ball (sight interference), a racket swing hinder (**backswing** swing, or **follow-through**), or a **safety hinder.** A safety hinder is called when a player stops play to avoid contact with another player that may cause an injury.

Point hinders, also known as **avoidable hinders,** are called when a player does not make a satisfactory attempt to allow an opponent full access to the return shot. This could include denying access to the ball, failing to move out of the way of the opponent's stroke, or blocking the path of the ball on a straight or cross-court shot angle. Also, intentionally obstructing or distracting an opponent's view of the ball (shouting, waving a racket, moving past the opponent's line of vision just before a shot attempt, etc.) or deliberately pushing an opponent during a rally is a point hinder.

This section is only a brief summary of some of the rules. For a complete list of the USRA rules, contact the USRA and request a copy of the official rule book.

dead-ball hinders
point hinders

court hinder
backswing
follow-through
safety hinder
avoidable hinders

COURT

Racquetball can be played in a four-wall, three-wall, or one-wall court. Three-wall and one-wall facilities are often built when finances are limited or where weather permits the use of outdoor facilities most of the year. The rules and techniques are similar in all courts, although strategy will change with the different court structures available for various shots. This book will deal primarily with the four-wall game.

Most indoor facilities will have a hardwood floor, although concrete is used occasionally. The court walls can be made of plastic-laminated panels, plaster, or even concrete. Glass-walled courts are becoming more popular but are very expensive to install and maintain. The courts should have recessed lighting fixtures and flush entry doors with recessed handles and hinges. Some courts will have an observation gallery in the upper area of the back wall where spectators can look down on the courts. The back wall of the court with a gallery will have the gallery opening at some point above the 12-foot minimum.

The specifications for court dimensions and markings are provided by the USRA. The standard four-wall court is 40 feet long, 20 feet wide, 20 feet high, and has a back wall at least 12 feet high. Court markings include the service line, the short line, the receiving line (not a solid line), the service box line, and the drive serve line.

The service zone covers the width of the court and is designated by the front edge of the service line and the back edge of the short line. The safety zone is the area behind the short line to the back edge of the receiving line. The service box is between the wall and the edge of the service box line nearest to the center of the court. The drive serve zone is the area between the wall and the edge of the drive serve line nearest to the center of the court (see figure 2.1).

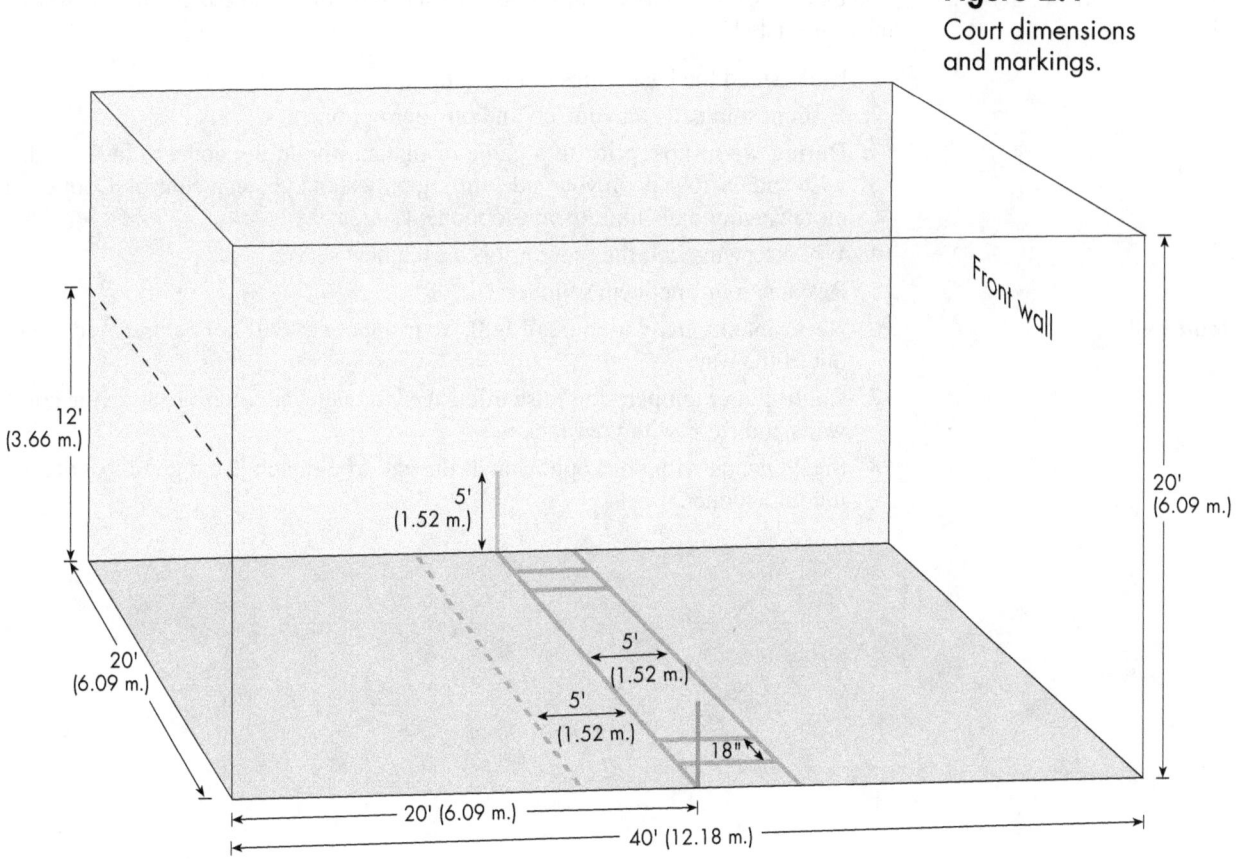

Figure 2.1
Court dimensions and markings.

SCORING

A regulation game of racquetball is played to fifteen points. Points are scored only by the server. If the receiver is unable to keep the ball in play, the server wins the rally and scores a point. No points are scored if the server loses the rally; the server becomes the receiver and the receiver now serves. The first player or team to score fifteen points wins the game. It is *not* necessary to win by two points. Match play is determined by the winner of two out of three games. In match play, the third game, if necessary, is played to eleven points.

ETIQUETTE

Most areas of etiquette in racquetball are covered under the rules of the game and are considered formal etiquette. Prominent items include the following:

1. Before serving, always wait until your opponent is in position and ready to receive the serve.
2. Always allow your opponent a path to the ball.
3. Always allow your opponent's shot a path to the wall.
4. Never jeopardize your opponent when trying to hit the ball. Use the hinder call to protect yourself and your opponent.
5. Never intentionally distract your opponent. Intentional distractions are against the rules and show poor sportsmanship.
6. If an unresolvable dispute arises when there is not a referee, replay the point. Afterward, clarify any questions on rules to avoid future disagreements.

SECTION TWO The Game

Informal etiquette includes items not necessarily mentioned in the rules section that are essential to an enjoyable experience on the racquetball court. A few of these are listed here:

1. Understand the basic rules of racquetball.
2. Be honest in calls on yourself and on your opponent.
3. During warm-ups, prior to a game or match, divide the court in half lengthwise and try to stay on your side, hitting only shots you can control. Cooperate on retrieving balls hit into your opponent's area.
4. When serving, call the score prior to each new serve.
5. Respect your opponent's hinder call.
6. Never intentionally hit a **dead ball.** Your opponent will not be prepared to get out of the way.
7. Control your temper; don't use offensive language, and don't beat up the court walls and floor with your racket.
8. Shake hands with your opponent at the end of a match. Be a good loser and a humble winner.

dead ball

SECTION 3

Skills and Drills

Section 3 will cover the rudimentary skills necessary to play a game of racquetball. The basic essentials of grip, wrist action, and stance, along with fundamentals of the forehand, backhand, and **overhead strokes** are discussed as Skill 1. Basic **offensive** and **defensive shots** are discussed as Skills 2 and 3. Skill 4 is the use of these forehand and backhand strokes to play shots rebounding off the back wall of the court. The serve and return of serve are explained as Skill 5, and advanced offensive and defensive shots complete the section as Skills 6 and 7.

overhead strokes
offensive and defensive shots

SKILL 1 Basic Strokes

Prior to this point, you have learned about racquetball equipment, game organization, warm-up and preparation to play, safety, and etiquette. Now you are ready to step onto the court and learn the basic skills that will enable you to play the game of racquetball.

The instructions in this book are written for right-handed players. Left-handed players will need to transpose most of these instructions to the opposite side for their use.

Grip

The grip is the foundation of every swing of the racket, and power, accuracy, and control are all affected by the grip. A proper grip will allow the wrist to produce maximum power. The racket face will be at the correct angle, and the palm and fingers will be able to control the racket during the stroke.

Forehand Grip

A forehand shot is an attempt to hit the ball from the side of the body where the racket hand is located. The "handshake" grip, or **Eastern forehand,** is the most popular forehand grip used in racquetball. Follow these steps to assume the handshake grip:

Eastern forehand

Figure 3.1

Reaching for handshake grip.

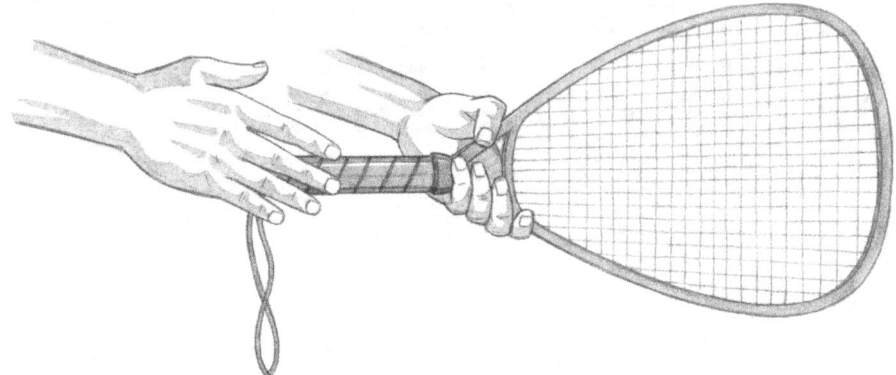

1. Take the racket in the left hand, extending the left arm, with the string surface perpendicular to the floor and the racket handle parallel to the floor.
2. Reach out with the right hand as though shaking hands, placing the palm of the right hand against the handle of the racket (see figure 3.1).

CUE: Holding too far up the handle reduces power and racket length.

3. The handle should lay diagonally across the palm of the hand with the end of the handle aligning with the heel of the palm (see figure 3.2a).

CUE: Holding the handle perpendicular to the fingers, rather than diagonally across the palm, reduces wrist action and power on most shots.

4. The V formed by the thumb and index finger should be along the top bevel (edge) of the handle (see figure 3.2b).
5. Wrap the fingers around the handle in a "trigger" position, with the index finger extended slightly (see figure 3.2c). The index finger assists with racket control and power when properly positioned. After positioning, wrap tip of "trigger finger" around racket handle (see figure 3.2b).

Figure 3.2

Handshake grip positioning.

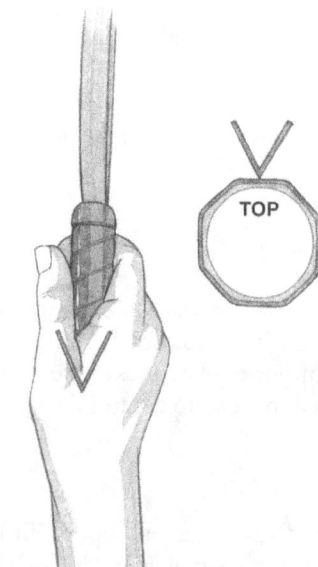

a Reverse angle with racket handle diagonally across the palm of the right hand

b V of thumb and index finger on top bevel

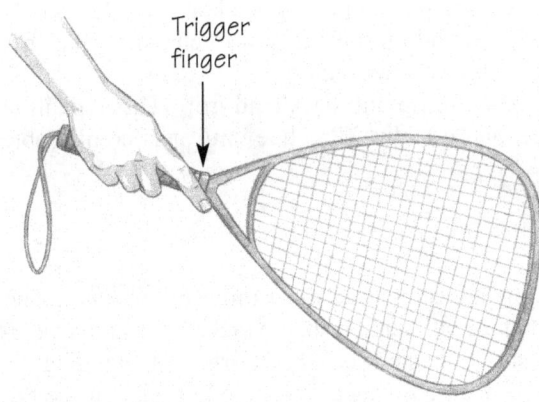

c Index finger as trigger finger

d Reverse angle with middle finger at the base of the thumb

Figure 3.2 Continued.

6. The middle finger should almost touch the palm at the base of the thumb as it curls around the racket handle (see figure 3.2d).
7. Check this grip for accuracy periodically, and it will soon become a comfortable habit on the court.

Backhand Grip

Many players, because of the speed of the ball and the limited reaction time, have started to adjust for a backhand stroke by simply rotating the wrist, setting the face of the racket parallel to the front wall at the **contact point** (see figure 3.3a). If there is time, players using the handshake grip on forehand shots may change their grip slightly to hit backhand shots (shots to the nonracket side of their body). The new position, called the Eastern backhand, can be achieved by following these steps:

1. Rotate the hand position slightly toward the thumb, aligning the thumb-index finger V on the top left bevel of the handle (see figure 3.3b).
2. Anticipate hitting a shot from the backhand side of the body early to allow more time to prepare the grip for that shot.
3. If time permits, use the thumb and fingers, or the nonracket hand, to rotate the racket clockwise one-eighth turn to align the V properly for the backhand attempt. If there is no time for one of these adjustments, rotate the wrist to place the racket face in the proper position.
4. After each backhand, remember to return to the proper handshake grip position for the next forehand shot.
5. Take time to practice the wrist rotation or these one- and two-handed grip adjustments until they become easy to execute consistently.

CUE: Failure to rotate the handshake grip for a backhand stroke usually results in the ball being hit higher than anticipated because the angle of the racket face is slightly upward.

contact point

Figure 3.3 Backhand grip adjustments.

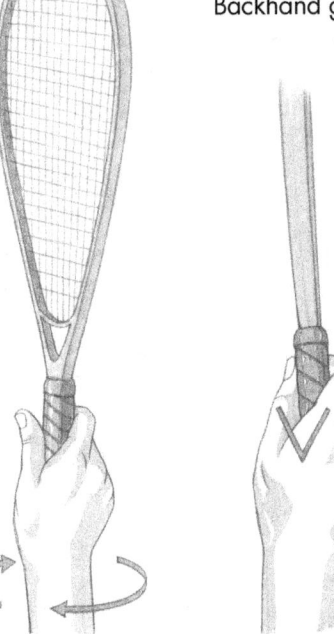

a Rotation of wrist from handshake grip

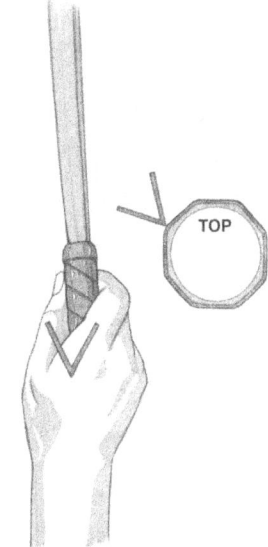

b Eastern backhand adjustment

continental grip

Failure to return to the handshake grip position after a backhand stroke usually results in the ball being hit into the ground on the ensuing forehand attempt because the angle of the racket face is slightly downward.

Practice changing between forehand grip and backhand grip. This repetition will make the switch more natural and effective. Practice until it is comfortable and comes naturally.

Continental Grip

An alternative grip not requiring any adjustment between forehand and backhand shots is the **continental grip.** With the continental grip, the racket is held in a position between the handshake grip and the Eastern backhand grip, not changing for either forehand or backhand. The V position is located on the left edge of the top bevel of the handle (see figure 3.4).

CUE: Adapt the wrist angle slightly for the different angles of the racket face, lowering for forehand shots and raising for backhand shots.

Overhead Smash or Western Grip

**overhead smash grip
Western grip**

When the ball has to be played above the shoulder, it can be difficult to contact the ball properly using either the handshake or the continental grips. The most common adjustment for playing these high attempts is the **overhead smash grip,** sometimes called the **Western grip.** This is achieved by rotating the racket counterclockwise (moving the hand position toward the fingers) until the V is located on the left edge of the right side of the racket handle (see figure 3.5A). Another way to find this grip position (but not during competition) is to lay the racket flat on the floor, then pick it up as you would a flyswatter, with the proper V placement.

This grip should never be used with a regular forehand or backhand shot. After using this grip for an overhead attempt, remember to adjust the grip properly for the next shot.

Figure 3.4
Continental grip.

Figure 3.5
Overhead smash or Western grip.

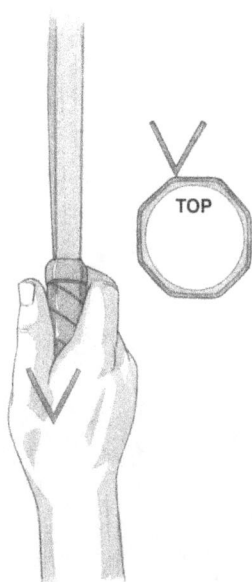

V on left edge of top bevel for Continental grip

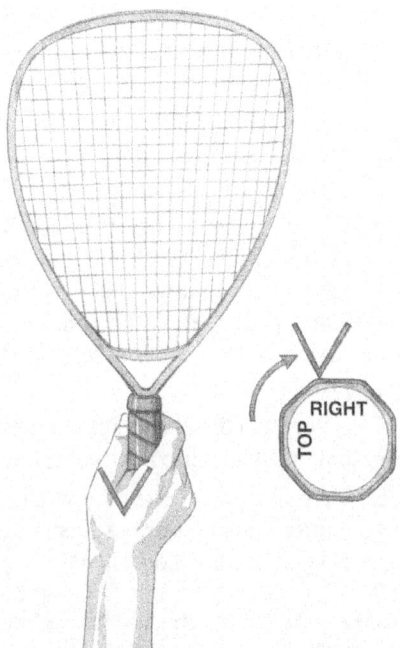

V on left edge of right side bevel

CUE: Never attempt to use the overhead smash grip on any other shots.

An improper grip will adversely affect the results of any shot attempt. Check the placement of the V frequently and adjust the grip when needed. Be conscious of always using the proper grip. This will result in more consistent and accurate shots. Table 3.1 lists common grip errors and methods for correcting these errors.

TABLE 3.1 Common Grip Errors: Cause and Correction

HANDSHAKE GRIP

Error	Correction
Forehand Grip	
1. Improper grip angle	1. Handshake grip
2. Wrong V location on handle	2. V in middle of top bevel
3. Choking up handle	3. Handle end on heel of palm
4. Handle perpendicular to fingers	4. Handle diagonal across palm
5. Index finger along back of handle	5. Trigger finger bent
Backhand Grip	
1. Same grip as forehand	1. Wrist rotation or Eastern backhand grip
2. No V change/too much change on Eastern backhand grip	2. V on top left bevel for Eastern backhand grip
3. Choking up handle	3. Handle end on heel of palm
4. Handle perpendicular to fingers	4. Handle diagonal across palm
5. Index finger along back of handle	5. Trigger finger bent
6. No grip adjustment for next stroke	6. Grip adjustment for next stroke

CONTINENTAL GRIP

Error	Correction
1. Wrong grip angle	1. Handshake grip
2. Wrong V location	2. V on left edge of top bevel
3. Choking up handle	3. Handle end on heel of palm
4. Handle perpendicular to fingers	4. Handle diagonal across palm
5. Index finger on back of handle	5. Trigger finger bent
6. No compensation for forehand/backhand differences	6. Wrist adjustment for differences in forehand/backhand strokes

OVERHEAD SMASH OR WESTERN GRIP

Error	Correction
1. Wrong grip angle	1. Flyswatter grip
2. Wrong V location	2. V on left edge of right side bevel
3. Choking up handle	3. Handle end on heel of palm
4. Handle perpendicular to fingers	4. Handle diagonal across palm
5. Index finger along back of handle	5. Trigger finger bent
6. No adjustment for next stroke	6. Grip adjustment for next stroke

Wrist Action

In racquetball, the action of the wrist is critical to the power of any shot. A stiff wrist will push the ball, creating very little force. The snapping of the wrist at the ball contact point generates much of the speed and power of racquetball. For any forehand or backhand stroke, the wrist must be cocked properly to create the desired power on that shot. More specific instruction will be given on wrist action for the forehand and backhand shots later in this section.

Loose Wrists Drill

To emphasize the importance of loose wrists and wrist action, perform the following drill:

1. Take the racket in a forehand grip.
2. Extend the right forearm, waist high, comfortably in front of the body.
3. With the left hand, hold the right forearm stationary.
4. Keeping the racket face perpendicular to the floor, repeatedly swing the racket forward and backward as far as possible, not moving the forearm.

Ready Position

ready position

The **ready position** is the ideal body position assumed prior to hitting any stroke except the serve. If possible, begin in this position before every shot, and return to it after every shot. To get into the ready position, face the front wall and spread the feet shoulder-width apart with the toes on the same plane. Shift the weight onto the balls of the feet and bend the knees. Lean forward slightly at the waist, and raise the racket to the front with the handshake or other chosen grip. The racket should be waist high, with the strings parallel to the sidewalls. The nonracket hand can be held free or can be touching the racket, ready to rotate the grip for an Eastern backhand, if needed. The neck is bowed up, holding the head so the eyes are able to follow the movement of the ball. Take a deep breath, anticipate the opponent's shot, and quickly move into position for the next stroke (see figure 3.6).

Figure 3.6
Ready position.

Front view   Side view

Forehand Stroke

The forehand stroke is used when hitting a ball on the same side of the body as the hand holding the racket. The forehand stroke, like every other stroke in racquetball, should begin from the ready position, progressing with proper footwork through the pivot position, the backswing, the forward swing, and the follow-through. The forehand is the most natural stroke action in racquetball and is the foundation of most participants' racquetball skill. The **drive shot,** a powerful shot hit with a forehand or backhand, is the most common shot in racquetball.

drive shot

CUE: When executing any shot in racquetball, always keep your eyes focused on the ball until you see the racket make contact with the ball.

Pivot/Footwork

The pivot and backswing occur simultaneously in preparation for the forward swing. After moving to the court location necessary to strike the ball at the proper contact point, pivot the body to a position facing the right sidewall. The feet should be comfortably spread apart with the weight on the instep of the right foot, similar to a batter's stance in baseball (see figure 3.7).

Two common errors on the pivot phase of the forehand stroke are as follows: (1) failure to pivot in preparation for the shot, and (2) keeping the weight on the front foot, instead of the back foot, after the pivot. In #1, the result is a "reach and slap" shot, with no opportunity to execute a proper swing at the ball. In #2, with the weight already shifted forward before the downward swing, much less power will be generated during the stroke.

Backswing

The backswing occurs simultaneously with the pivot while moving into position to contact the ball.

CUE: Raise the racket and cock the wrist while moving to the contact point, or the arm and racket will not be ready for the downswing.

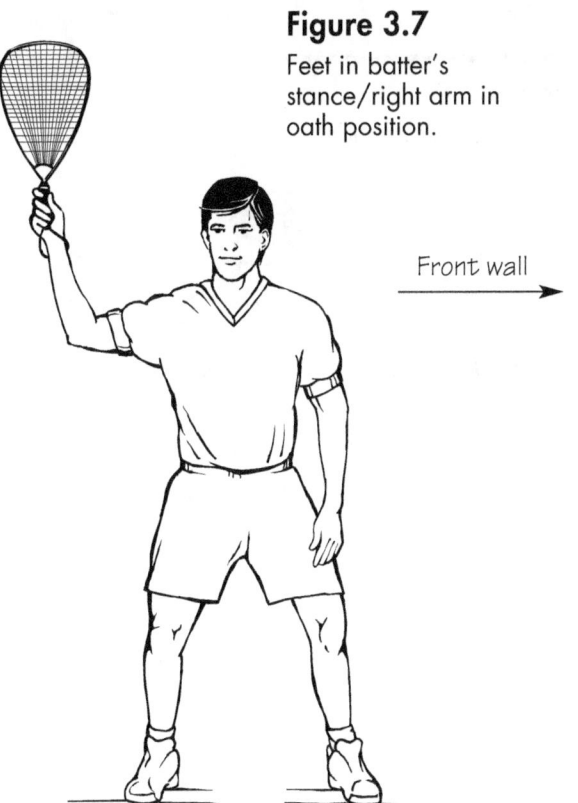

Figure 3.7
Feet in batter's stance/right arm in oath position.

Front wall →

Raise the right arm in the backswing to the "oath" position (see figure 3.7), with the wrist cocked and the racket tip pointed at, or just above, the right ear (see figure 3.8). To cock the wrist properly, bend the wrist toward the thumb side, and slightly to the back, of the hand (see figure 3.8). For power, twist the trunk of the body by rotating the left arm and shoulder forward as the right arm is raised for the backswing.

Three common errors in the backswing are as follows: (1) failure to draw the arm and racket back while moving into position for the ball, (2) holding the racket too low at the top of the backswing, and (3) extending and locking the wrist and elbow at the top of the backswing. In #1, this lack of preparation often results in a hurried, short swing, where the racket is pulled back and then forward in an awkward, jerky motion, without time to do either backswing or forward swing properly. In #2, the downswing will be much shorter and, consequently, much less power will be generated. In #3, the

Figure 3.8
Wrist position on backswing.

Wrist cocked for forehand stroke

Close-up of wrist angle

downswing will be a stiff-armed tennis stroke from the shoulder only, producing good ball control but limited power.

Forward Swing or Stroke

After pivoting into position and raising the arm properly on the backswing, the forward swing is ready to be executed. The footwork, trunk rotation, and arm action happen simultaneously to correctly perform the forward swing. Firmly push forward from the inside of the right foot, shifting the weight to the left foot while stepping to the contact point. As the left foot steps, it should be turned to a 45 degree angle to the sidewall, allowing the body to rotate easily during the follow-through. Keep the right foot planted on the floor through the forward swing. The heel will rise on the follow-through, but do not take the ball of the foot off the court until returning to the ready position. While the weight is shifting, slightly open the left shoulder and hip to the front wall (see figure 3.9). At the same time, the right arm and racket begin their downward motion, led by the elbow. The arc of the racket is curved downward to the level of the ball and then moves flat toward the ball, as though "moving across a tabletop" (see figure 3.10a). The elbow leads the forearm and racket through the arc until just prior to ball contact, where the elbow has become almost fully extended (see figure 3.10b). At this point the wrist "snaps" and the elbow fully extends, producing maximum racket speed at ball contact (see figure 3.11a). The knees should be bent sufficiently to allow the racket to reach the ball at the lowest possible contact point, without dropping the **racket head** below the level of the hand. Keep the racket face parallel to the front wall and the racket handle almost parallel to the floor through the contact point (across the tabletop) (see figure 3.11b). *The ideal contact point for a forehand stroke* is directly between the left knee and the right sidewall, with the right arm and racket fully extended as close to the floor as possible (see figure 3.11c/d). A powerful forward swing will result in a drive shot, a ball hit on a straight, flat line to the front wall that rebounds quickly into the court.

Six common errors on the forward swing result in loss of power and/or accuracy on the shot: (1) rotating the wrist instead of snapping it, also called "slicing," (2) scooping the ball instead of hitting it flat (off the table-

Figure 3.9
Open hip and shoulder to front wall.

top), (3) swinging from the shoulder with the wrist and elbow extended (tennis swing), (4) hitting the ball too close to the body so the arm cannot be fully extended at the contact point, (5) shifting the weight from left foot to right foot during the downswing, and (6) striking the ball at the wrong position in relationship to the ideal contact point.

In #1, refer to the loose wrists drill for proper wrist action. The improper action occurs when the wrist is rotated clockwise and the racket face is turned at an upward angle (instead of being held parallel to the front wall) through the contact point (see figure 3.12a). The resulting hit will have a twangy sound (instead of a clear ping or pop), and the ball may travel in an upward arc from the racket face (instead of a flat line-drive angle). In #2, the ball is lifted at an upward angle and hits high on the wall and often to the left side of the court because the knees were not bent and the player did not hit flat through the contact point (see figure 3.12b). In #3, the player may have control on the shot but will not be able to generate a lot of power with no wrist or elbow snap. In #4, the player has moved too close to the ball, and on the downward swing, the elbow is jammed into the rib cage, not allowing the arm to swing freely through the

Figure 3.10
Arc of forward swing.

a Tabletop arc with contact point

b Elbow extended, wrist cocked, knees bent prior to contact point

Figure 3.11
Contact point.

a Wrist snap at contact point

b Racket level stays the same through contact point

c Front view of contact point

d Overhead view of contact point

Figure 3.12
Two common errors on forward swing.

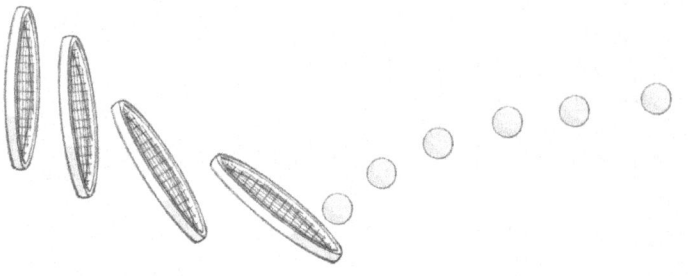

a Rolling wrist and racket slicing

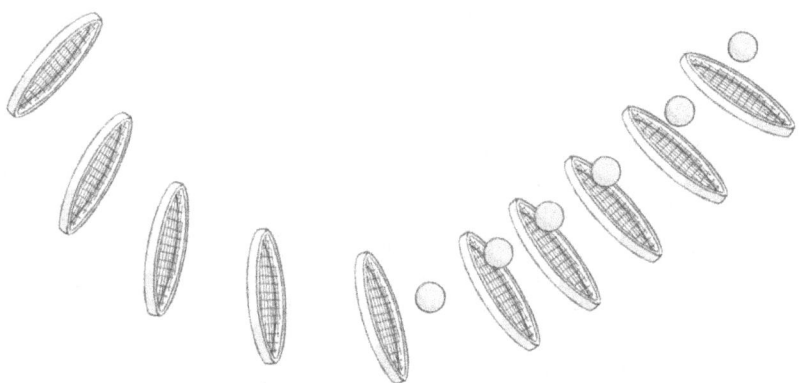

b Scooping without bending the knees

range of motion necessary for a proper stroke. In #5, most of the power is lost because the lower body is taken out of the force, and the ball is often lofted because the racket face is turned at an upward angle on the swing as the weight shifts backward. In #6, striking the ball too high, such as waist or chest level, almost always results in a rebound shot that bounces high and is easily returned during a rally. Striking the ball behind the ideal contact point reduces power because the wrist and elbow snap are taken out of the swing, and the racket face angle may drive the ball downward. Striking the ball in front of the ideal contact point may cause the ball to be lofted and often results in the ball being pulled to the left side of the court.

Figure 3.13
Forehand follow-through.

Follow-through

The follow-through is the final phase of the mechanics involved in the forehand stroke. After striking the ball, many beginning players make the mistake of forgetting to follow-through, or finish, their forehand stroke, thereby reducing their power and accuracy. The follow-through is executed by continuing with the racket on the tabletop angle after striking the ball, until the fully extended right arm rises in an upward arc and finishes with the racket just above the left shoulder. The left arm and shoulder will be fully rotated, opening the chest to the front wall and allowing the right arm to complete its long arc. The knees will be pointing in the direction of the front wall, and the player will be prepared to move quickly into a ready position for the next shot (see figure 3.13).

Three common errors on the follow-through include the following: (1) stopping the racket at the **contact point** with the ball without completing the stroke, (2) pulling the racket too quickly to the left shoulder, and (3) straightening the knees too quickly and standing up while still in contact with the ball. In #1, the ball is punched or pushed and most of the power is lost. It is also more difficult to return to the ready position without a proper follow-through. In #2, the player throws the left shoulder and arm back and forces the right arm to pull to the left too quickly, pulling the racket face and the ball to the left side of the court. Another cause of error #2 is the failure to open the chest and left shoulder to the front wall, forcing the racket face to the left too quickly. In #3, the player will often scoop the shot if he or she straightens up too soon at the bottom of the downswing (see figure 3.12b).

contact point

Table 3.2 summarizes the mechanics involved in the forehand stroke.

TABLE 3.2 Forehand Stroke Fundamentals

PIVOT

1. Turn to face right sidewall.
2. Shift weight to right instep in batter's stance.

BACKSWING

1. Raise arm and racket in oath position.
2. Cock wrist to thumb side, slightly back.
3. Point racket tip at or above right ear.
4. Rotate trunk with left shoulder forward.

FORWARD SWING

1. Shift weight to left foot at contact point.
2. Angle the left foot 45 degrees at contact point.
3. Open the left shoulder and hip to front wall.
4. Begin the downward movement of the arm and racket.
5. Lead with the elbow on the downswing.
6. Arc the racket across a tabletop toward the ball.
7. Contact the ball between left knee and right sidewall.
8. Fully extend right arm and racket close to the floor.
9. At contact point, snap wrist and fully extend elbow.
10. Keep the racket face parallel to front wall, racket handle parallel to floor through the contact point (tabletop).

FOLLOW-THROUGH

1. Continue on the tabletop until arm rotation forces racket to finish the arc above the left shoulder.
2. Fully open the chest to the front wall.
3. Point the knees toward the front wall.
4. Return to the ready position for the next shot.

Figure 3.14
Backhand stroke.

a   Backswing position

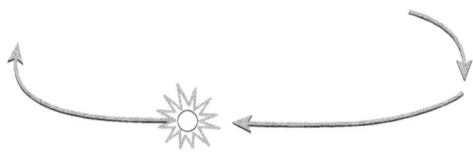

b   Forward swing tabletop arc for backhand stroke

c   Body position at contact point for backhand stroke

Backhand Stroke

The backhand stroke is used when hitting a ball on the opposite side of the body as the hand holding the racket. The backhand stroke is similar to the forehand in many ways. Like the forehand, it should begin from the ready position and progress through the pivot position, the backswing, the forward swing, and the follow-through. The upper body mechanics of the backhand stroke are not natural motions and will require a learned action. A solid backhand stroke is essential to a well-rounded game of racquetball.

Pivot/Footwork

The pivot and backswing, as in the forehand, occur simultaneously in the backhand stroke. After moving to the court location for the proper contact point, pivot the body to a position facing the left sidewall. The feet should be comfortably spread apart, with the weight on the instep of the left foot, ready for the forward swing.

Common errors for the backhand pivot are the same as in the forehand pivot.

Backswing

The backswing occurs simultaneously with the pivot, while moving into position to contact the ball. Draw the right arm across the body, bringing the right hand to the level of and slightly behind the left shoulder. Cock the wrist to the palm side and slightly toward the thumb, with the racket tip pointed above the back of the head. Pull the right shoulder toward the left side, twisting at the waist for potential power on the forward swing (see figure 3.14a).

d   Follow-through position with racket above right shoulder

CUE: As in the forehand, raise the racket and cock the wrist while moving into the contact position, or the arm and racket will not be ready for the downswing.

Common errors for the backhand backswing are the same as for the forehand backswing.

Forward Swing or Stroke

After the player has pivoted into position and raised the arm properly on the backswing, he or she can execute the forward swing. The footwork, trunk rotation, and arm/racket action must happen simultaneously to correctly perform the forward swing. Push off from the inside of the left foot, shifting the weight to the right foot while stepping to the ball contact point. As the right foot steps, it should be opened at a 45 degree angle to the sidewall, allowing the body to rotate easily during the follow-through. Keep the left foot planted on the floor during the forward swing. The heel will rise on the follow-through, but keep the ball of the foot on the court until returning to the ready position. Because of the location of the right arm across the body, the chest and shoulders will remain parallel to the sidewall throughout the downward motion of the forward swing. The hips will open slightly toward the front wall, and the knees will point toward the left front corner of the court at the contact point. At the same time, the right arm and racket make their downward motion. Similar to the forehand stroke, the arc of the swing will have a flat, tabletop bottom section through the contact point and into the follow-through (see figure 3.14b). The elbow leads the forearm and racket through the arc until just prior to ball contact, where the elbow is almost fully extended. At this point, the wrist snaps and the elbow fully extends, producing maximum racket speed and power on ball contact (see figure 3.14c). Once again, the knees should be bent sufficiently to allow the racket to reach the ball at the lowest possible contact point, without dropping the racket head below the level of the hand. Keep the racket face parallel to the front wall and the racket handle parallel to the floor through the contact point. *The ideal contact point for a backhand stroke* is 6 to 12 inches in front of the right knee toward the front wall and a racket length away from the knee toward the left sidewall. The right arm and racket are extended and reach as close to the floor as possible.

CUE: Do not attempt to run around the ball and hit a forehand instead of a backhand. All balls between the player and the left sidewall are backhand shots.

Four common errors on the forward swing in the backhand include the following: (1) striking the ball without using any wrist snap (locked wrist), (2) using only wrist action without swinging the arm, and (3) not extending the elbow on the swing. In #1, the wrist is locked into position and does not produce any power. This error often doubles up with #3 and is hit like a tennis backhand. Refer to the loose wrists drill for proper wrist action. In #2, the arm and upper body are left out of the swing, and the racket is slapped at the ball. This results in a weak return shot. In #3, failure to extend the elbow reduces power and often results in the ball being pulled crosscourt to the right corner or sidewall. Error #4 occurs when a player has no confidence in hitting a backhand stroke and, instead, tries to hit a forehand whenever possible.

Follow-through

The follow-through is the final phase of the mechanics of the backhand stroke.

CUE: Remember to finish all strokes in racquetball with the appropriate follow-through.

After contacting the ball, the racket will continue through the contact point on the tabletop. It will rise at the end of the arc to a level above the right shoulder, with the tip pointing at the right ear or above the head. The chest and shoulders will open to the front wall, and the hips will turn with the upper body. The knees will rotate toward the front wall, allowing the player to return to the ready position for the next shot (see figure 3.14d).

Three common errors in the backhand follow-through are as follows: (1) stopping the racket at the point of contact without completing the stroke, (2) pulling the right shoulder, right arm, and racket toward the right sidewall on contact with the ball, and (3) straightening the knees too quickly on contact with the ball. In #1, the ball is punched or pushed and most of the power is lost. In #2, the ball is pulled to the right and control and accuracy are minimal. In #3, the ball is usually lofted, resulting in an easy return shot in the rally.

Table 3.3 summarizes the mechanics involved in the backhand stroke.

Table 3.4 lists common forehand and backhand stroke errors and methods for correcting these errors.

TABLE 3.3 Backhand Stroke Fundamentals

PIVOT

1. Turn body to face left sidewall.
2. Shift weight to left instep in batter's stance.

BACKSWING

1. Move right arm/racket across body; right hand to left shoulder.
2. Cock wrist to palm side, slightly toward thumb.
3. Point racket tip above back of head.
4. Pull right shoulder toward left side of body.

FORWARD SWING

1. Shift weight to right foot while stepping to contact point.
2. Angle right foot 45 degrees, right hip open to the front wall.
3. Begin the downward movement of the arm and racket.
4. Arc the racket across the tabletop to contact point.
5. Contact the ball in front of right knee toward the front wall.
6. At contact point, snap wrist and fully extend elbow.
7. Keep racket face parallel to front wall and handle parallel to floor through contact point (tabletop).

FOLLOW-THROUGH

1. Continue on the tabletop through contact point.
2. At end of arc, raise racket to level above right shoulder, with tip pointing at, or above, right ear.
3. Open chest, shoulders, and hips to front wall.
4. Point knees to front wall.
5. Return to ready position for next shot.

TABLE 3.4	Forehand and Backhand Stroke Errors: Cause and Correction
ERROR	**CORRECTION**
A. Pivot	
1. Failing to pivot	1. Pivot to face sidewall
2. Keeping weight on front foot	2. Shift weight to back foot
3. Using poor positioning for contact point	3. Adjust positioning for ideal contact point on stroke
B. Backswing	
1. Holding racket too low	1. Raise arm to oath position (forehand)
2. Keeping a straight elbow and wrist	2. Use oath position/cock the wrist
3. Not twisting trunk for power	3. Pull front shoulder toward chin
C. Forward swing	
1. Shifting weight to back foot on downswing	1. Push off back foot instep and shift weight to front foot
2. Pulling front shoulder toward chin on downswing	2. Open shoulder and chest to front wall on downswing
3. Scooping ball, hitting high on front wall	3. Bend knees, use tabletop arc on downswing
4. Using tennis swing: straight elbow and wrist through downswing	4. From oath position, extend elbow and snap wrist at contact point with ball
5. Striking ball behind ideal contact point	5. Position deeper in court or use better timing on downswing
6. Striking ball in front of ideal contact point	6. Position closer to front wall or use better timing
7. Striking ball at chest level	7. Adjust position for lower contact point on ball
8. Striking ball too close to body	8. Position farther away from ball to force extended elbow at contact point
9. Straightening knees too quickly at contact point	9. Keep knees bent and use tabletop arc through ball
10. Rolling wrist on downswing	10. Snap wrist as in Loose Wrists Drill
11. Not keeping eyes on ball through contact point	11. Watch ball until it leaves racket surface on contact
D. Follow-through	
1. Failing to follow-through	1. Allow racket and arm to finish tabletop arc and open chest to front wall
2. Pulling racket too quickly to left side of body after contact point	2. Do not throw front arm and shoulder toward sidewall too soon.

TROUBLESHOOTER'S GUIDE

Ball going too high: C1; C3; C6; C9; grip
Ball going too low, hitting floor before front wall: C5; grip
Need more power: A1; A2; B1; B2; B3; C2; C4; C8; C10; D1
Hitting into stroke-side sidewall: A1; A3; C5; late backswing
Hitting into opposite sidewall: C1; C2; C6; D2
Ball always rebounds for easy return by opponent: C7; see "Ball going too high" causes; strategy
Missing ball on swing: A3; C11

Forehand and Backhand Drills/Self-Tests

Shadow Drill: Basic forehand and backhand without a ball

1. Begin in the ready position.
2. Pivot toward the proper sidewall for a forehand or backhand stroke. Raise the backswing while pivoting.

CUE: Check foot position, weight distribution, arm location and angle, and wrist cock at the top of the backswing.

3. Step toward an imaginary contact point, downswing, and follow-through.

CUE: Check knee bend, tabletop angle of racket arc, open chest to front wall, lead with elbow, arm extension and wrist snap at contact point, proper follow-through, return to ready position.

4. Repeat forehand and backhand sides until comfortable with the fundamentals.

Forehand Stroke with Ball Drill: Use toss/drop and sidewall toss.

1. Begin in the pivot position, facing the right sidewall, with the right arm and racket raised in the backswing.
2. Toss/drop a ball softly, about 2 feet in front of the left foot and 3 feet toward the sidewall, that will bounce about 2 feet off the floor (see figure 3.15a).
3. Step toward the contact point with the front foot and strike the ball off the bounce with a proper downswing and follow-through (see figure 3.15b).

CUE: Check foot position, downswing technique, contact point, follow-through, and return to ready position.

4. Repeat drill, tossing ball softly off the right sidewall to the proper contact point. Evaluate fundamentals.

Figure 3.15
Overhead views of drills.

 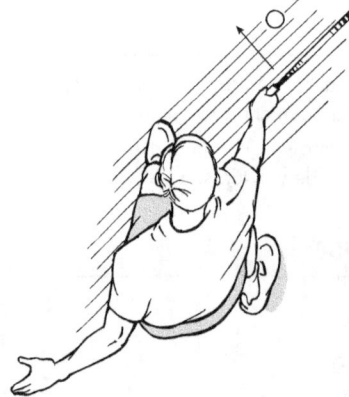  

a Overhead view of forehand drop point

b Overhead view of forehand contact point

c Overhead view of backhand drop point

d Overhead view of backhand contact point

Backhand Stroke with Ball Drill: Use toss/drop and sidewall toss.

1. Begin in the pivot position, facing the left sidewall, with the right arm and racket raised in the backswing.
2. Toss/drop a ball softly, about 2 feet in front of the right foot and 2 feet toward the sidewall, that will bounce 2 feet off the floor (see figure 3.15c).
3. Step toward the contact point and strike the ball as it bounces, using the proper downswing and follow-through (see figure 3.15d).

CUE: Check foot position, downswing technique, contact point, follow-through, and return to ready position.

4. Repeat drill, tossing ball softly off left sidewall to proper contact point. Evaluate fundamentals.

Partner Forehand and Backhand Drill: Use front wall toss or hit.

1. Subject begins in the ready position in center court, 8 feet behind the short line. The forehand partner aligns as in figure 3.16a.
2. The partner tosses or hits a ball off the front wall that will rebound to the proper court position for the subject to strike the ball using a forehand stroke.
3. The subject moves to the proper court position, pivots to the right sidewall, and strikes the ball with a forehand stroke. The ball should be hit flat and hard, with a low contact point, to the front wall.
4. The subject returns to ready position after stroke.
5. Evaluate fundamentals.

CUE: Check foot position, foot movement, and stroke fundamentals.

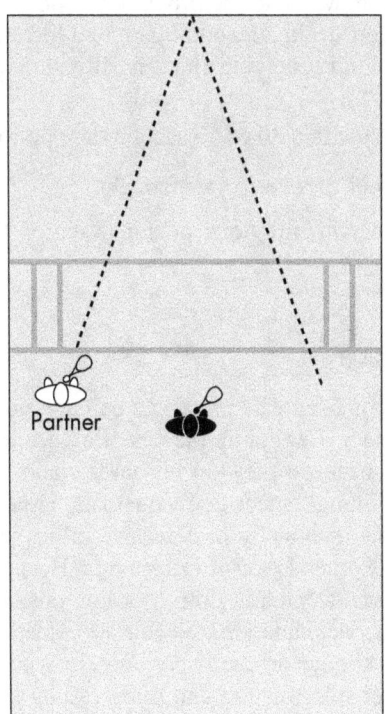
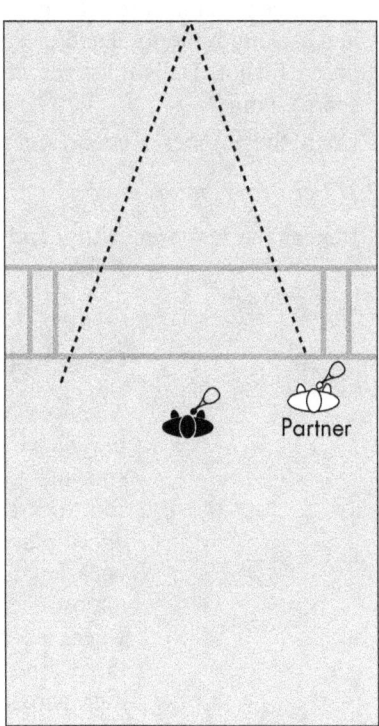

Figure 3.16
Partner forehand and backhand drills.

a Alignment for partner forehand drill

b Alignment for partner backhand drill

6. Repeat drill and evaluation from backhand stroke alignment (see figure 3.16b).
7. Difficulty can be increased by adjusting set-up placement and requiring front wall accuracy on the return stroke.

Partner Forehand and Backhand Beginner's Self-Test

Court preparation: Divide the front wall into four equal vertical (floor to ceiling) sections, with a line across the wall 5 feet from the floor (see figure 3.17). Each section will be numbered as indicated.

1. Set up for forehand or backhand as in "Partner Forehand and Backhand Drill."
2. Partner will set up subject for eight (or twelve, time permitting) forehand shots. On each shot, the subject will attempt to hit the ball into a predetermined section of the front wall. Two (or three) shots should be attempted at each section. A score of 6 (or 9) indicates a 75 percent accuracy performance.

CUE: *Check foot position, foot movement, and stroke fundamentals.*

3. Repeat for backhand stroke.
4. Practice the forehand and backhand shots until able to accomplish a score of 75 percent or higher.

Advanced Forehand and Backhand Rally Drill and Self-Test

1. Begin in a forehand stroke position, about 8 feet in front of the back wall and in the middle of the court.
2. Toss the ball off the sidewall and begin the rally with a forehand stroke to the front wall.
3. Continue to return the ball on each rebound. Move to the proper court position and use either the forehand or the backhand stroke, depending on ball location on each shot. Balls must be hit from behind receiving line on rally shots to score a point.
4. Count the number of successful returns made in a 30 or 60 second time period.

CUE: *Check foot position, foot movement, and stroke fundamentals.*

5. Repeat the test frequently, and compare with previous personal scores for improvement.

Figure 3.17
Beginner's self-test for forehand and backhand.

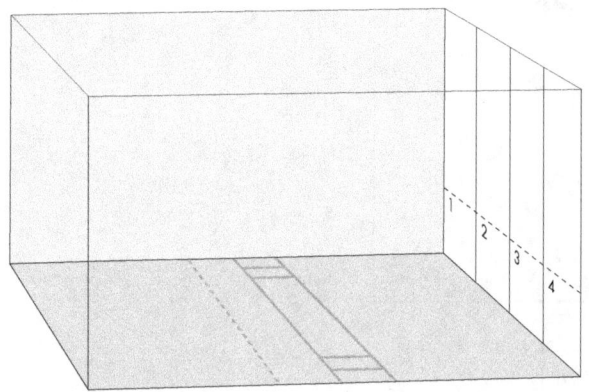

Overhead Stroke

The overhead stroke is used when hitting a ball at a position above the shoulder. Beginning players often use this shot too frequently because they do not understand the footwork and positioning aspect of racquetball. Experienced players use it strategically in defensive rallies and occasionally for an overhead pass or kill attempt. Because almost every ball will eventually drop to a low position where a forehand or backhand stroke could be effective, the overhead stroke should be used sparingly. It is not a high percentage offensive weapon and often results in a set-up return for your opponent if not hit accurately. The overhead stroke should be developed only after becoming proficient at the forehand and backhand strokes.

The overhead stroke uses the overhead smash grip, also referred to as the Western grip. Like every other stroke in racquetball, the overhead stroke should begin from the ready position and progress with proper footwork through the backswing, the forward stroke, and the follow-through.

Footwork/Pivot

Move to the court location necessary to strike the ball properly, called the contact point. In the stroke stance, the right foot should point toward the front right corner, while the left foot should point almost directly to the front wall (see figure 3.18a). The left foot should be placed comfortably in front of the right foot, and they should be spread far enough apart to provide for good balance. The weight should be evenly distributed between both feet. This position is similar to the throwing position used when tossing a ball overhand. The only pivot action that occurs is when the upper body twists slightly during the backswing phase of the stroke.

Two common errors on the footwork/pivot phase of the overhead stroke are as follows: (1) keeping the feet parallel with each other, as in the ready position, and (2) pivoting completely to face the right sidewall, as in the forehand stroke. In #1, the result is a reach and slap shot, with no opportunity to execute a proper swing at the ball. In #2, the ball can be pushed or punched forward, but a proper stroke cannot occur because the body is blocking a proper contact point and follow-through motion.

Backswing

In the backswing, the right arm and racket should be raised while moving into position to contact the ball. Once the feet are set and the speed of the approaching ball is determined, the racket should be held in a "back-scratcher" position behind the shoulders and between the shoulder blades. The elbow should be bent at about a 90 degree angle and point toward the ceiling, with the wrist cocked back. The shoulders and chest should be pivoted toward the right sidewall for power. The eyes should be watching the ball closely. The weight should be shifted back to the right foot. The left arm should be used for balance (see figure 3.18b).

Two common errors on the backswing phase of the overhead stroke are as follows: (1) failure to pivot the chest and shoulders toward the right sidewall, and (2) failure to raise the elbow and drop the racket into a back-scratcher position. In #1, limited power will be generated with the stroke because of the lack of body rotation during the forward swing. In #2, the stroke will be much shorter, and consequently, much less power will be generated. The ball will be punched or pushed, but a proper stroke will not be executed.

Forward Swing or Stroke

After assuming the backswing position, the forward stroke is ready to be executed. Shift the weight forward with a small step of the left foot. At the same time, begin the arm and racket action by pulling the elbow forward as you extend the arm. Rotate the chest and shoulders to face the front wall at the contact point. The wrist should snap forward and the elbow become fully extended at the contact point, which is at full arm and racket extension height and about a foot in front of the forehead (see figure 3.18c). This is also referred to as the "throwing motion." The angle of the racket face will determine the type of overhead shot being executed with the stroke.

Two common errors on the forward swing are as follows: (1) punching at, or pushing the ball, and (2) not shifting the weight to the front foot during the forward swing motion. In #1, good ball control is possible, but very little power can be generated. In #2, accuracy will be reduced, and it will produce a short swing with very little power.

Figure 3.19
Overhead stroke.

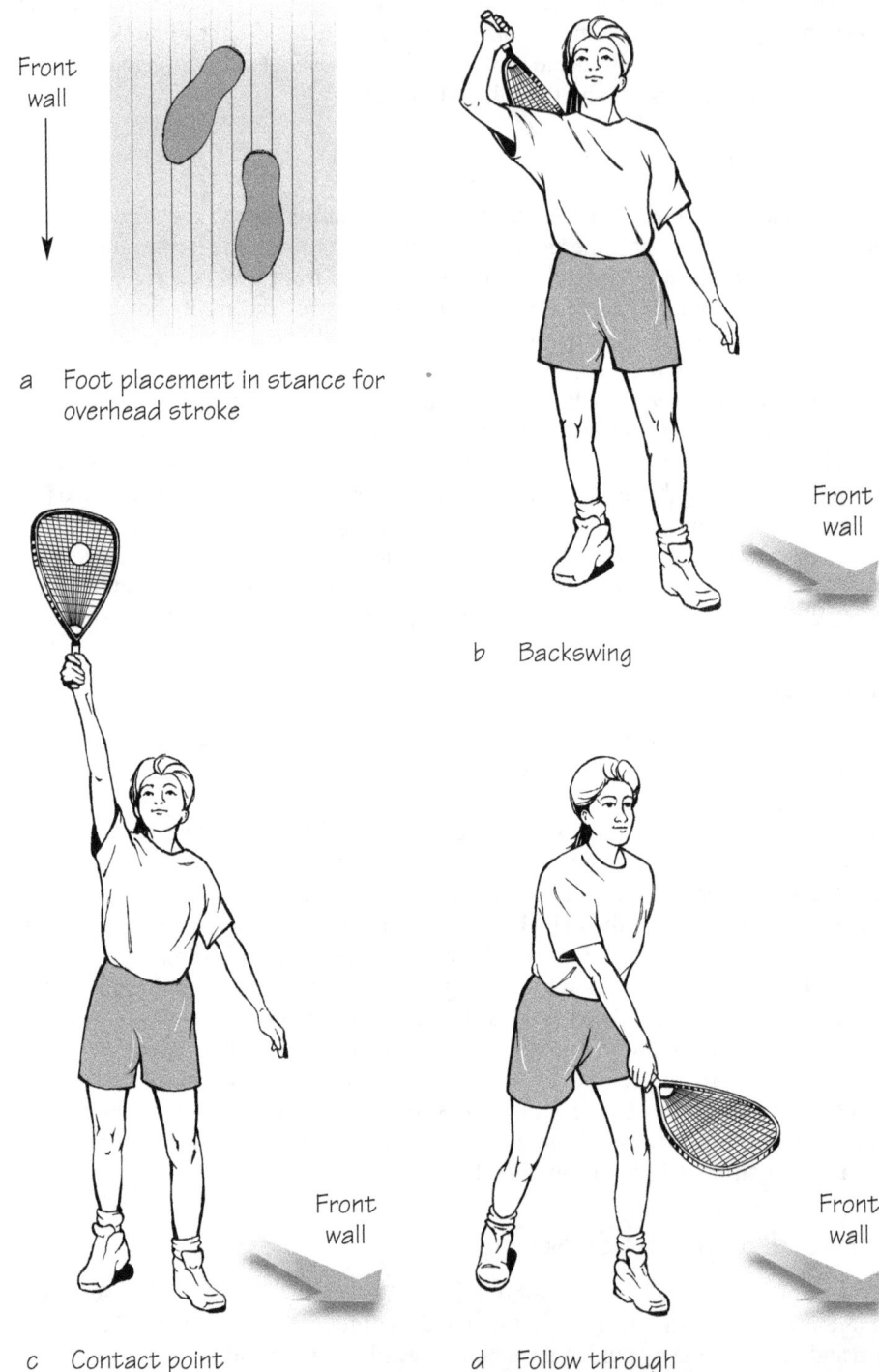

a Foot placement in stance for overhead stroke

b Backswing

c Contact point

d Follow through

Follow-through

The follow-through is important to the total stroke because it continues the momentum built during the forward stroke, allowing the racket to swing "through the ball" at the contact point. This produces the maximum power available with the forward swing. The follow-through also helps bring the player back to a ready position to prepare for the next shot. The swinging motion should continue on its natural arc, and the racket should finish the follow-through close to the left hip. The shoulders should be parallel to the front wall and the feet pointed at the front wall (see figure 3.18d).

Two common errors on the follow-through are as follows: (1) stopping the follow-through too quickly after the contact point, and (2) stepping too far forward with the right foot after contact with the ball. In #1, this detracts from the power of the shot and can cause elbow and arm problems, such as tennis elbow and tendinitis. In #2, the player loses balance and cannot recover to center court and the ready position quickly.

Table 3.5 summarizes the mechanics involved in the overhead stroke.

Table 3.6 lists common overhead stroke errors and methods for correcting these errors.

TABLE 3.5 Overhead Stroke Fundamentals

FOOTWORK

1. Point right foot to right corner/left foot to front wall.
2. Balance weight in throwing position.
3. Do not pivot to either sidewall.

BACKSWING

1. Hold racket in back-scratcher position.
2. Bend elbow 90 degrees, pointed toward ceiling.
3. Cock wrist back.
4. Turn shoulders and chest to right sidewall.
5. Shift weight to right foot.

FORWARD SWING

1. Shift weight to left foot.
2. Pull elbow forward and extend arm.
3. Pivot chest and shoulders to face front wall.
4. Contact the ball 1 foot in front of forehead and at full arm and racket extension height.
5. Snap wrist forward at contact point.
6. Fully extend arm and racket at contact point.
7. Combine #1–#6 for a throwing motion.
8. Adjust racket face angle to determine shot placement.

FOLLOW-THROUGH

1. Allow racket to continue on natural arc.
2. Finish racket arc close to left hip.
3. Point feet at front wall.
4. Return to the ready position for the next shot.

TABLE 3.6 Common Overhead Stroke Errors: Cause and Correction

ERROR	CORRECTION
A. Footwork/Pivot	
1. Pointing feet at sidewall	1. Point right foot to right corner, left foot to front wall
2. Balancing weight on front foot	2. Balance weight evenly
3. Pivoting to sidewall	3. Do not pivot/face front wall
B. Backswing	
1. Extending racket to side or too high	1. Hold racket in back-scratcher position
2. Extending elbow straight up or to right side	2. Bend elbow 90 degrees, point at ceiling
3. Keeping a stiff, straight wrist	3. Cock wrist back
4. Not rotating upper body	4. Rotate chest to right sidewall
5. Balancing weight on both feet or on front foot	5. Shift weight to back foot
C. Forward Swing	
1. Not shifting weight forward	1. Shift weight to left foot
2. Maintaining stationary elbow position	2. Pull elbow forward/extend arm
3. Not rotating chest	3. Rotate chest to front wall
4. Contacting the ball at improper point for desired shot angle	4. Contact ball 1 foot off forehead/full extension height
5. Not snapping wrist on contact	5. Snap wrist at contact point
6. Bending elbow at contact point	6. Extend elbow at contact point
D. Follow-through	
1. Stopping racket/punching at ball	1. Continue racket on its arc
2. Holding racket high after shot	2. Finish arc near left hip area
3. Pointing feet at sidewalls	3. Point feet at front wall
4. Not being ready for next return	4. Return to ready position/center court

Overhead Stroke Drills

Tennis Drill: Basic overhead stroke.

1. Begin in center court position, about 6 to 8 feet behind the short line and in the middle of the court.
2. Hold a ball in the left hand and get into the backswing position.
3. With an open left palm, toss the ball about 3 feet high and about a foot in front of your forehead.
4. As the ball drops to the proper contact point, use good overhead stroke technique to hit a flat, hard return to the front wall.
5. Repeat drill until comfortable with the fundamentals.

Overhead Stroke off Front Wall Drill: Basic overhead stroke.

1. Begin in center court position, about 6 to 8 feet behind the short line and in the middle of the court.
2. Toss or hit a ball high off the front wall to set up an overhead stroke attempt.
3. Move to the proper position, and execute the overhead stroke using good fundamentals. Hit the ball flat and hard to the front wall on the return.
4. Repeat drill, moving the ball around court to add more difficulty to the footwork and positioning for the stroke.

Partner Overhead Stroke Drill: Use front wall toss or hit.

1. Align as illustrated for Partner Forehand and Backhand Drill in figure 3.16.
2. The partner tosses or hits the ball off the front wall to rebound high enough for the subject to hit an overhead stroke.
3. Subject moves to the proper court position and hits an overhead stroke, hard and flat, to the front wall. A target area may be established to measure accuracy as the participants improve on this skill.
4. The subject returns to the ready position.
5. Evaluate fundamentals.
6. Repeat drill as needed.

SKILL 2 — Basic Offensive Shots

Offensive shots are those shots designed to aggressively end a rally. Every player should practice these shots and become proficient at them before they can be effectively used in a game situation. One drawback to attempting most offensive shots is that if the player does not hit the shot correctly, the rebound will set up the opponent to attempt an offensive shot of his or her own. This is why fine-tuning these skills by practice and repetition is so important.

When attempting an offensive shot, keep in mind your opponent's strengths and weaknesses on the court. If your opponent has a particularly strong forehand game or weaker backhand skills, hit more balls to his or her backhand side. This forces your opponent to hit returns that may result in more opportunities for you to hit offensive shots to end the rally.

We will cover two types of basic offensive shots: the **passing shot** and the **kill shot.** Each can be very effective if executed properly and used in the appropriate situation on the court.

passing shot
kill shot

Passing Shots

Passing shots, as the name implies, are meant to get the ball past your opponent on the court. If hit correctly, the ball will pass by your opponent and **die** in the backcourt rather than rebounding off the back wall to give him or her a second chance at the ball. Passing shots are most effective when your opponent is caught in the frontcourt or midcourt area or is out of position to one side of the court or the other.

die

CUE: Learn the angles necessary to direct the ball to particular areas of the court.

Passing shots utilize drive shot fundamentals and may be hit with a forehand or a backhand stroke, as discussed under "Skill 1 Basic Strokes."

The most common errors made when hitting passing shots are as follows: (1) improper angle selection, (2) the use of too much power, or (3) hitting the ball too high off the front wall. The first error results in the ball returning to center court for an easy return shot by your opponent. Hitting at proper angles will prevent this error. The last two errors often result in the ball rebounding off the back wall, again creating opportunities for your opponent to make a return shot. Contacting the ball at a lower point, hitting lower off the front wall, and adjusting the power used to strike the ball will reduce these two errors.

down-the-wall pass

There are three types of passing shots: the **down-the-wall pass,** the crosscourt pass, and the crosscourt sidewall pass.

Down-the-wall Pass

wallpaper pass

The down-the-wall pass is also known as the **wallpaper pass.** It is the most frequently used passing shot. It consists of hitting the ball directly to the front wall with sufficient force to pass your opponent on the rebound, and having the rebound travel close to and parallel with the near sidewall into the backcourt area (see figure 3.19a). It should be hit low enough to die in the backcourt, eliminating a back wall rebound opportunity. When the ball dies will also depend on the force of the shot.

frontcourt

The most effective times to use a down-the-wall pass are when your opponent is in the **frontcourt** area (see figure 3.19b), in the center court (see figure 3.19c), or out of position toward the opposite sidewall (see figure 3.19d). Do not hit a down-the-wall pass attempt when your opponent is positioned to the same side of the court or is in the backcourt area. A forehand stroke should be used to hit the ball down the forehand sidewall, and a backhand stroke should be used to hit the

Figure 3.19
Down-the-wall pass.

a   Down-the-wall pass
(also down-the-wall ceiling shot)

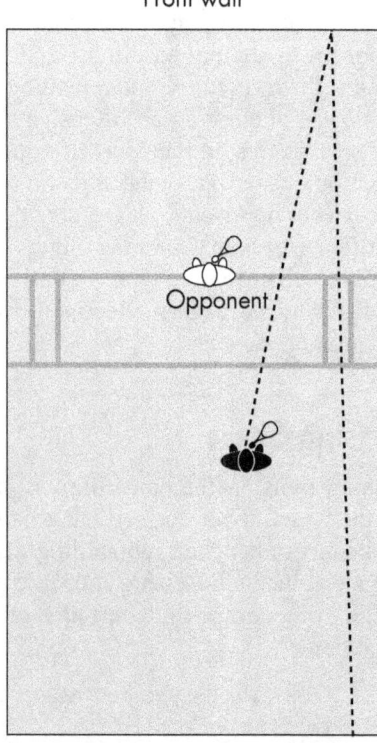

b   Down-the-wall pass
with opponent in frontcourt

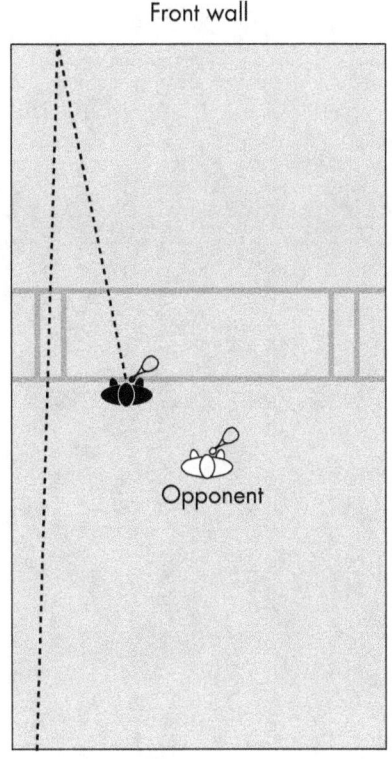

c Down-the-wall pass
with opponent in center court

d Down-the-wall pass
with opponent toward court sidewall

Figure 3.19
Continued.

ball down the backhand sidewall. An overhead may be used from either side, but the downward angle of the shot may make it difficult for the ball to die in the backcourt area.

Crosscourt Pass

The crosscourt pass is also a popular shot in racquetball. It consists of hitting the ball at an angle to the front wall and having the ball rebound in a V-line toward the opposite back corner of the court (see figure 3.20a). Hitting the sidewall deep in the corner may help take some velocity off of the ball, allowing it to die in the back corner. As with other passing shots, the force and height of the shot should not allow your opponent a back wall rebound opportunity.

The most effective time to hit a crosscourt pass is when you and your opponent are on the same side of the court (see figure 3.20b). The angle of the shot depends on your court position and your opponent's position. These vary with every rally situation; therefore, you must learn to judge and control the angle of your shot to successfully hit crosscourt passing shots. A strong forehand stroke hit crosscourt to an opponent's backhand will often result in a weak return or will end the rally.

Crosscourt Sidewall Pass

The crosscourt sidewall pass (also called the wide-angle pass) is similar to the crosscourt pass with one exception: it is designed to hit the sidewall at the same court depth as your opponent (see figure 3.20c). This will make it difficult for your opponent to cut off the ball as it travels down the side of the court. Hitting the side-

Figure 3.20
Crosscourt pass.

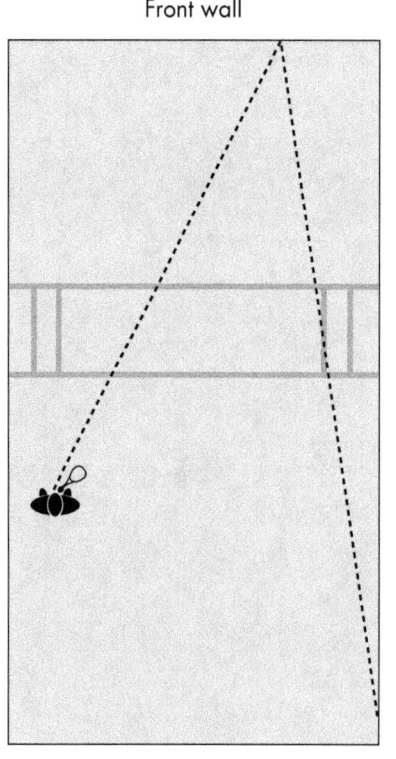

a Crosscourt pass
(also crosscourt ceiling shot)

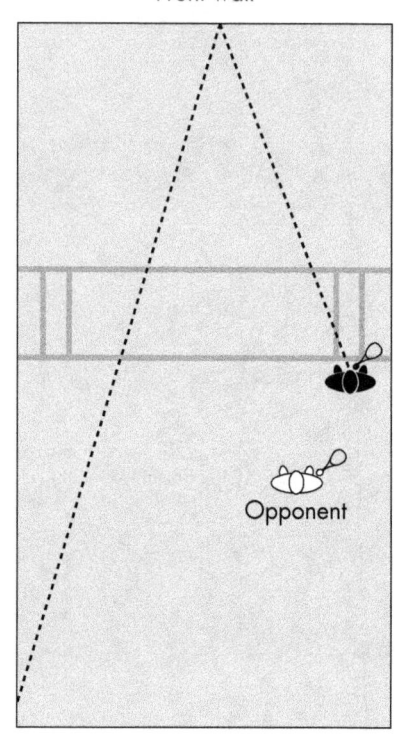

b Crosscourt pass
with opponent on same side of court

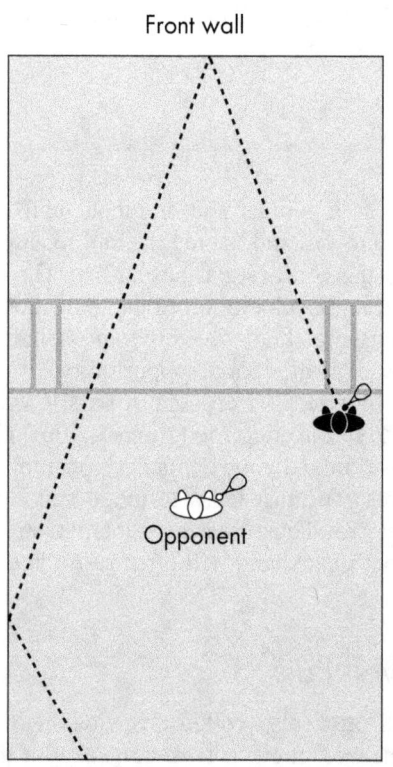

c Crosscourt sidewall pass

TABLE 3.7	Passing Shot Summary
PASSING SHOTS	**ERRORS**
1. Choose low contact point.	1. Contacting too high.
2. Hit low on front wall.	2. Hitting too high on front wall.
3. Hit with sufficient power.	3. Hitting too hard/too soft.
4. Base shot angles on opponent's court position.	4. Using improper angles on shots.

wall also slows the speed of the ball and makes it less likely to produce a back wall rebound opportunity. This is the most difficult passing shot to master but is also the most effective when properly executed.

Learn the correct angles to hit these shots effectively. Each situation will be slightly different, so be aware of the relationship between your court position and that of your opponent. Hit the shot most likely to pass your opponent and result in a winner for you. You do not have to be pinpoint accurate to effectively use passing shots to score points and win rallies. Keep your opponents off balance by mixing up your shot selection and forcing them to cover the most court surface to return your shots. And when they set you up for a good offensive return, use these passing shots or one of the following kill shots to "put it away."

Table 3.7 lists the fundamentals of the passing shot, as well as common errors.

Passing Shot Drills

Down-the-wall Drill: Use for both forehand and backhand practice.

1. Begin in the right side of the court for forehand and the left side of the court for backhand.
2. Using good stroke technique, drop the ball and hit down the near sidewall, within approximately 2 feet of the wall (see figure 3.19a). Try not to hit the sidewall with the ball, except deep in the court near the back wall. Do not hit the shot high or hard enough to allow a playable rebound off the back wall before the second bounce (see figure 3.21).
3. To be proficient with this shot, practice this technique until you can be accurate more than half the time (6 out of 10) with the shot.
4. Repeat the drill, tossing the ball off the sidewall for the shot setup.
5. Repeat the drill, having a partner toss or hit the ball off the front wall for the shot setup.
6. To increase accuracy and awareness of shot placement on the front wall, tape three 24-inch squares on the front wall, 18 inches off the floor (see figure 3.21). Put one square in the middle of the wall for use later in the Crosscourt Passing Shot Drill, and position the outside edge of the other two squares approximately 4 feet from each sidewall. Use the two outside targets during practice sessions to help you learn the correct angles for each down-the-wall passing shot.

Crosscourt Passing Shot Drill: Forehand and backhand practice.

1. Practice from various spots on the court. Hit from either side, using both forehand and backhand strokes. Also, vary your depth in the court from the short

Figure 3.21
Down-the-wall pass.

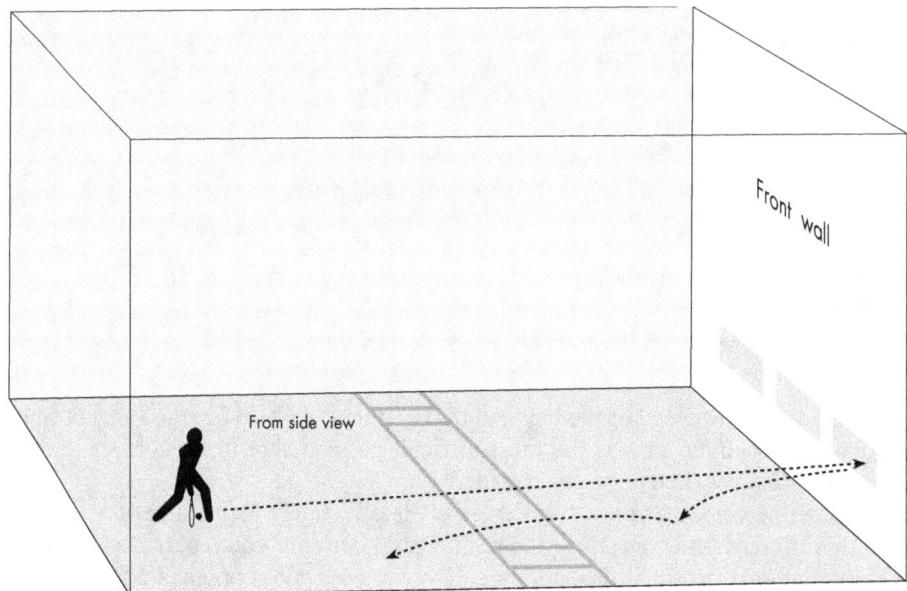

line to the back wall. Learn the front wall contact angles necessary to put the ball in the crosscourt corner (see figures 3.22a and 3.22b).

2. Using good stroke technique, drop the ball and hit a crosscourt passing shot. Your objective is to have the ball rebound off the front wall and go deep into the backcourt corner area, at an angle within 3 feet either side of the corner/sidewall crotch. Do not hit the shot too high or too hard, causing the ball to rebound off the back wall before the second bounce.
3. To be proficient with this shot, practice this technique until you can be accurate more than half the time (6 out of 10) with the shot.
4. Repeat the drill, tossing the ball off the sidewall for the shot setup.
5. Repeat the drill, having a partner toss or hit the ball off the front wall for the shot setup.
6. Use the squares from the Down-the-Wall Drill setup to help determine the proper angles for these shots.

Crosscourt Sidewall Passing Shot Drill: Forehand and backhand practice.

1. Use the same format as the Crosscourt Drill except for the aiming point and shot angles.
2. Hit the ball at an angle to the front wall that will result in a rebound to the sidewall within 3 feet of the receiving line marker, either on the fly or after a bounce (see figures 3.23a and 3.23b). Do not hit the shot too high or too hard, causing the ball to rebound off the back wall before the second bounce.
3. To be proficient with this shot, practice these techniques until you can be accurate more than half the time (6 out of 10) with the shot.

Kill Shots

Kill shots are the most effective way to end a rally when properly executed. A kill shot, hit low and hard, will bounce twice before an opponent has an opportunity to make a return shot. The body position for any kill shot includes bending at the knees and dropping the hips toward the floor to get to the proper "low" position.

Skills and Drills SECTION THREE 47

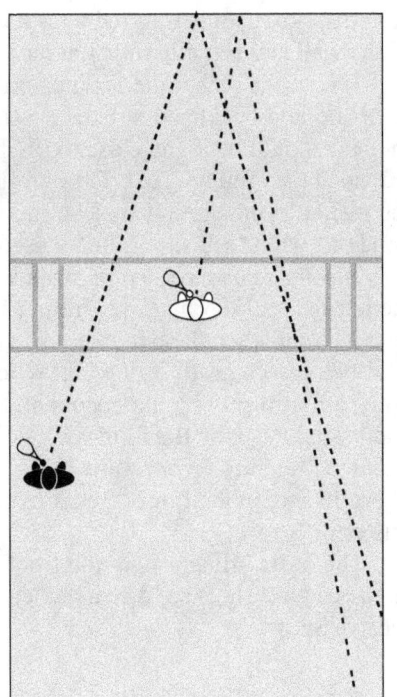

a   Angles from right side   b   Angles from left side

Figure 3.22
Crosscourt pass angles.

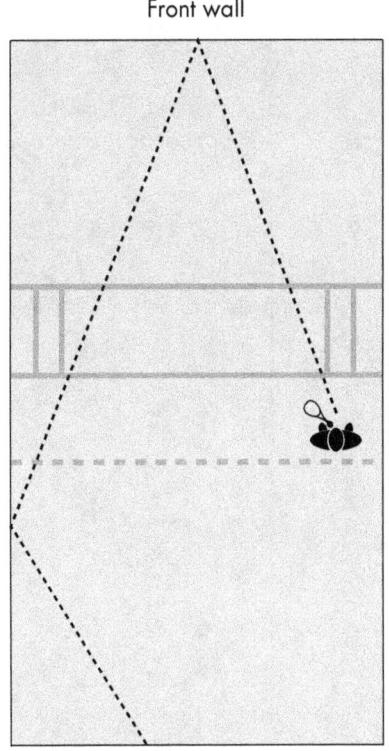
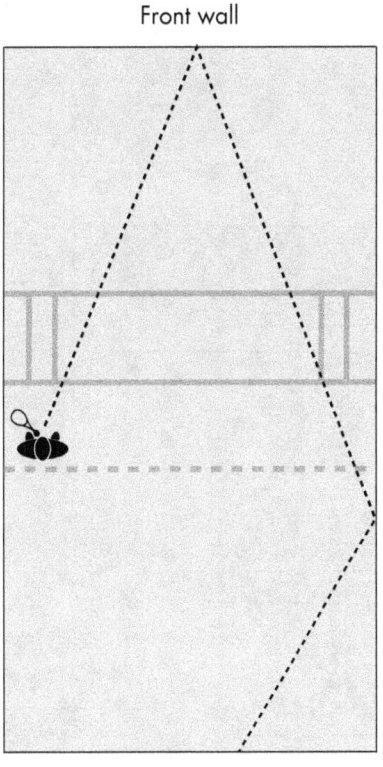

a   Angles from right side   b   Angles from left side

Figure 3.23
Crosscourt sidewall angles.

CUE: Do not just bend over at the waist to make low contact with the ball.

rollout

A perfect kill shot is referred to as a **rollout,** where the ball is hit to the exact base of the wall and actually rolls flat on the floor as it rebounds off the wall surface.

The stroke technique for most kill shots comes from the fundamentals of the forehand and backhand strokes described as "Skill 1" in section 3. Contact with the ball should be made close to the floor, with the knees bent and the racket arm extended (see figure 3.24). The ball should travel in a straight line from the face of the racket to the aiming spot on the wall, close to the floor. The aiming spot depends on which kill shot is being used.

The most common errors made when hitting kill shots are as follows: (1) contacting the ball too high, (2) hitting the front wall too high, and (3) hitting a kill shot attempt when the opponent is in excellent position to return the rebound. The first two errors result in the ball rebounding high enough and/or deep enough to allow a return shot by the opponent. Making contact with the ball at a lower point and hitting lower on the front wall will prevent these two errors from occurring frequently. The third error results in the opponent being able to return the shot, possibly a kill shot of their own. Better placement or a different shot strategy will reduce this error.

pinch kill

The basic kill shots are the front wall kill, the corner kill, and the **pinch kill.** Advanced kill shots are discussed later in this section under "Skill 6 Advanced Offensive Shots."

Front Wall Kill Shot

The front wall kill, appropriately named, is a kill shot directly to the front wall that is aimed to rebound and contact the sidewall deep in the backcourt area. The ball is hit from a low contact point with a flat, powerful stroke to a spot *within 12 inches or less of the floor on the front wall* (see figure 3.24a). The closer to the floor that

Figure 3.24
Front wall kill shots.

a   Side view

b   Front wall kill with opponent in backcourt

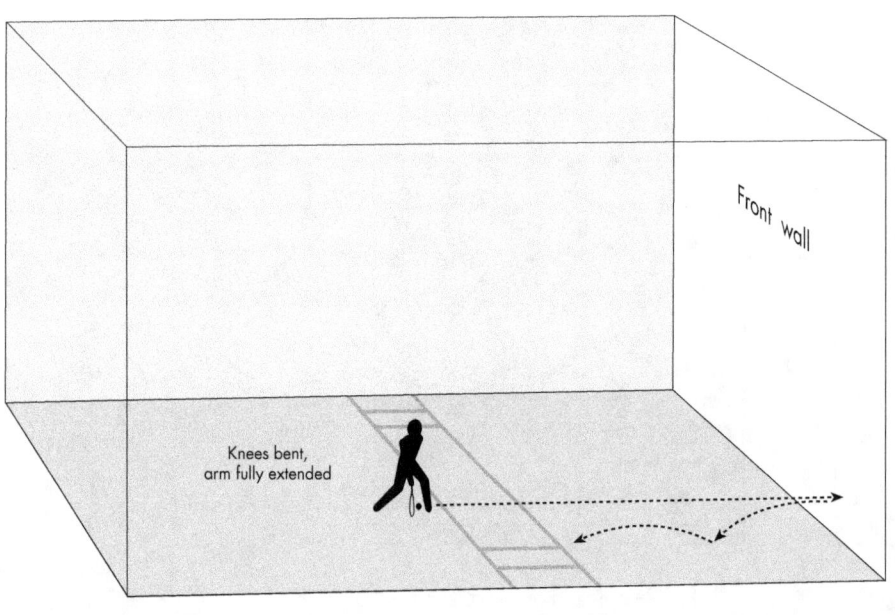
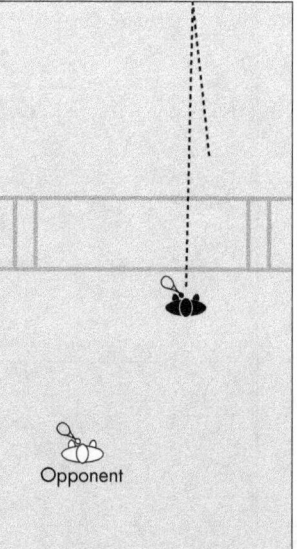

the ball hits the front wall, the better the opportunity for a successful kill shot. The ball will rebound off the front wall and almost immediately hit the floor. The spot of the second bounce will end the rally and is dependent upon how high the ball hits on the front wall and the force applied to the stroke.

The strategy for kill shot placement should be similar to passing shot strategy, depending on your court position and the position of your opponent. The angles at which front wall kill shots are hit should resemble the angles of the passing shots (see figures 3.19, 3.20, and 3.23), resulting in the ball rebounding away from your opponent's court position. This is because the ball, if hit too high for a successful kill shot, still may pass your opponent and end the rally. If your opponent is deep in the backcourt area, a middle front wall kill is also an excellent choice (see figure 3.24b), because the ball will bounce twice before a return shot can be hit.

Corner Kill Shot

The corner kill is executed by contacting the ball using the same technique as with a front wall kill. The aiming point for this kill shot is low on the front wall and within 1 to 2 feet of the front wall-sidewall crotch. This causes the ball to immediately rebound into the sidewall and down to the floor. The quick second bounce, ending the rally, will depend on the height and force of the shot. The rebound angle off the sidewall will return the ball to the midcourt area, opposite where the shot originated (see figures 3.25a and 3.25b). The racket face must be adjusted at the ball contact point to direct the ball at the appropriate angle into the corner area. This shot, as with any kill shot, must be hit low and hard to successfully end the rally.

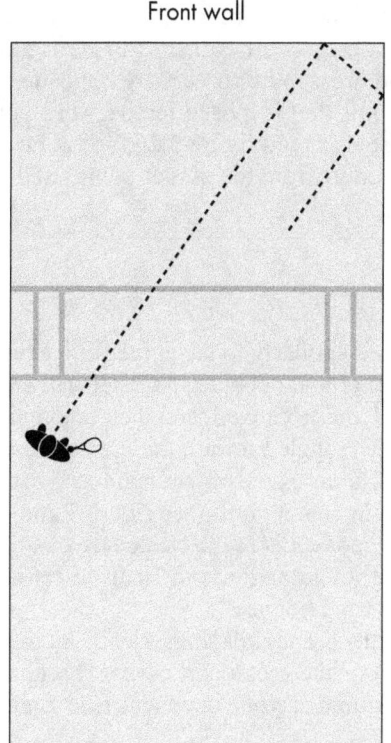
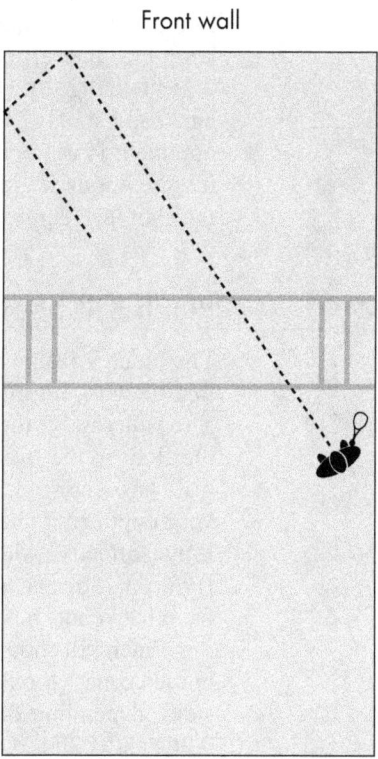

a   Corner kill from left side   b   Corner kill from right side

Figure 3.25
Corner kill shots.

Figure 3.26
Front wall kill shots.

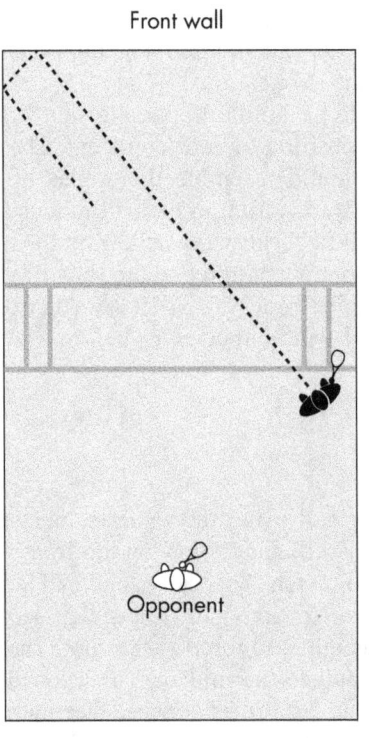
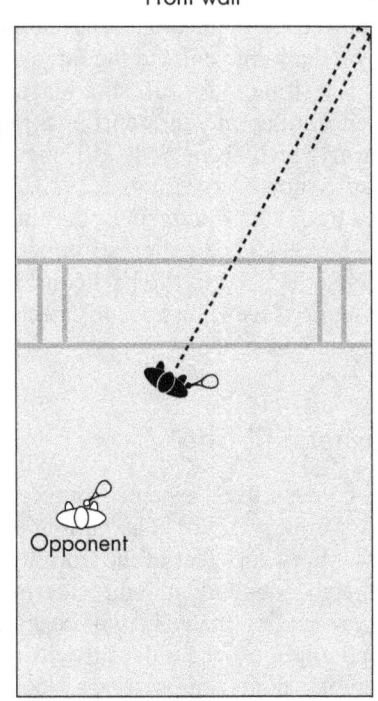

a Corner kill shot

b Corner kill shot with opponent favoring opposite side

Figure 3.27
Pinch kill shot.

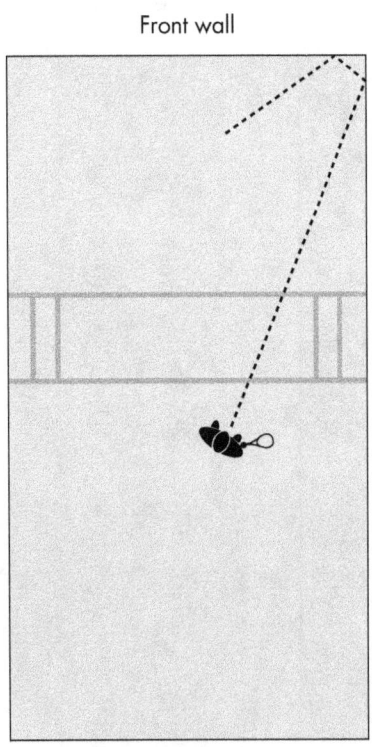

There are two types of corner kill shots. Hitting a forehand into the right corner is called a home corner kill. Hitting a forehand into the left corner is a crosscourt corner kill (see figures 3.25a and 3.25b). Home and crosscourt corners are opposite for backhand shots. The corner kill shot is most effective when your opponent is in the backcourt area (see figure 3.26a) or is favoring the opposite side of the court from the corner being used on the shot (see figure 3.26b).

Pinch Kill Shot

The pinch kill shot is executed similarly to the corner kill, except that the ball, hit into the corner area, contacts the sidewall first. The ball will hit the sidewall, the front wall, and then rebound to the floor in the frontcourt area, angled toward the opposite sidewall (see figure 3.27). This is an excellent strategic shot when your opponent is beside you in center court (see figure 3.28a). It is also effective when your opponent is in the backcourt area (see figure 3.28b) because the rebound angle is difficult to retrieve from backcourt before the second bounce.

Pinch kill shots, as with the corner kill shots, can be hit to the home corner (forehand side) or the crosscourt corner (backhand side), depending on the position of your opponent (see figures 3.28c and 3.28d).

Table 3.8 lists the fundamentals of the kill shot, as well as common errors.

Skills and Drills SECTION THREE 51

Figure 3.28
Pinch kill shot strategy.

a   Left corner with opponent beside you

b   Right corner with opponent in backcourt

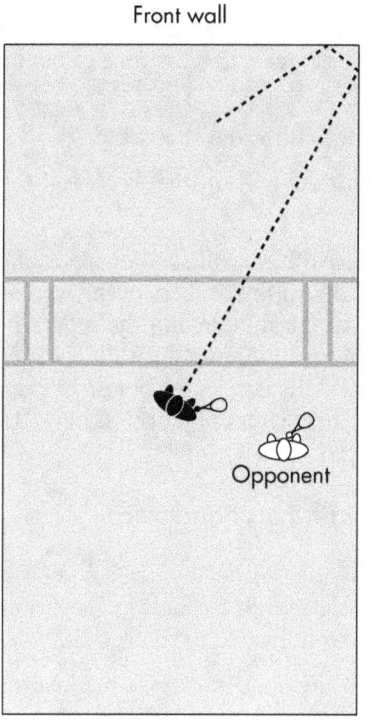

c   Right corner (home corner) with opponent beside you

d   Left corner (crosscourt corner) with opponent between wall and you

TABLE 3.8 Kill Shot Summary

KILL SHOTS	ERRORS
1. Choose low contact point.	1. Contacting too high.
2. Hit ball low and flat.	2. Hitting ball too high.
3. Hit with sufficient power.	3. Hitting too hard/too soft.
4. Use proper shot selection.	4. Allowing rebound to be playable by opponent.
5. Use proper shot placement.	5. Using improper shot placement.

Kill Shot Drills

Front Wall Kill Shot Drill: Forehand and backhand practice.

1. Use an imaginary line, or put a tape line across the front wall, 12 inches up from the floor.
2. Hit from various spots in the backcourt area.
3. Using good stroke technique, emphasize getting low by bending the knees and dropping the hips. (Don't just bend over at the waist.) Also emphasize hitting the ball low and flat to the front wall.
4. Drop the ball and hit front wall kill attempts, contacting the ball within 12 inches of the floor. Keep the shot at or below that 12-inch level as it travels to the front wall.
5. To be proficient with this shot, practice this technique until you can be successful at hitting at or below the 12-inch line at least half the time (5 out of 10) with the shot.
6. Repeat the drill, tossing the ball off the sidewall for the shot setup.
7. Repeat the drill having a partner toss or hit the ball off the front wall for the shot setup.
8. To add another element of control, place five ball canisters, or other targets, along the base of the front wall (see figure 3.29). Space them evenly across the court, with one in the middle and the others 3 feet apart. Repeat the drill, attempting to hit a specific canister with each kill shot. Three out of 10 is an excellent score for this "target practice" skill.

Figure 3.29
Front wall kill drill.

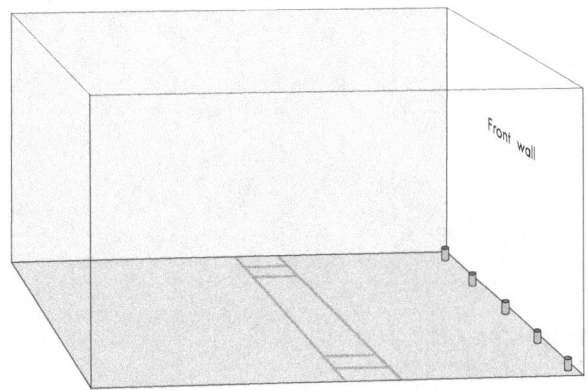

Ball cans for targets

Corner Kill Shot Drill: Forehand and backhand practice.

1. Mark the court with a 2-foot box in the front and sidewall corners as indicated in figure 3.30.
2. Hit from each of the court positions marked in figure 3.31.
3. As in the Front Wall Kill Shot Drill, use good stroke technique and emphasize getting low and hitting the ball low and flat.

4. Drop the ball and hit corner kill shot attempts, contacting the ball within 12 inches of the floor. Attempt both home corner and crosscourt corner kill shots. Keep the shot at or below that 12-inch level as it travels to the front wall. Attempt to hit the ball within the 2-foot target boxes in the front wall corners, remembering that closer to the floor and the sidewall is better.
5. To be proficient with this shot, practice this technique until you can be successful at hitting the target box at least half the time (5 out of 10) from each spot indicated in figure 3.31.
6. Repeat the drill, tossing the ball off the sidewall for the shot setup.
7. Repeat the drill, having a partner toss or hit the ball off the front wall for the shot setup.

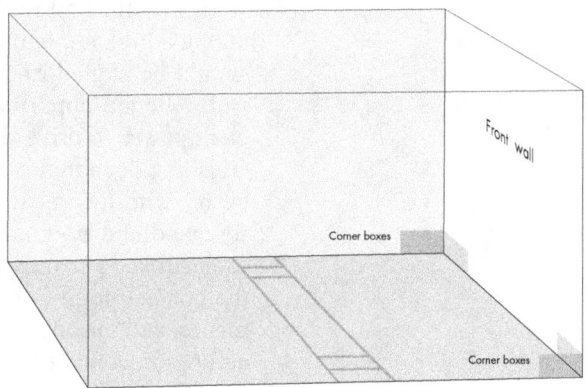

Figure 3.30
Corner and pinch kill drill.

Pinch Kill Shot Drill: Forehand and backhand practice.

1. Repeat instructions from Corner Kill Shot Drill, but hit into the sidewall box first instead of the front wall box, as explained in the Corner Kill Shot Drill (see figure 3.30).

SKILL 3 Basic Defensive Shots

Defensive shots are designed to place the ball in a court position that will prevent an opponent from hitting a return shot that will win the rally. Their purpose is not to score points and end rallies. Defensive shots are primarily used when the player does not have a good setup for a kill or passing shot, which occurs when the ball can be played only at a high contact point. When a player attempts a kill or passing shot from a high contact point, the results are often a setup for an offensive shot by the opponent. By selectively using defensive shots in your strategy, you will not allow your opponents to hit winning shots on their returns. These shots force the opponent to hit returns that will keep the ball in play, giving you another opportunity to win the rally. Defensive shots are also used to force a player out of center court position who may be dominating the game from that area or to fatigue an opponent by forcing him or her to run and move around the court. Players should master one or more defensive shots to give them some important versatility in their shot repertoire.

When attempting a defensive shot, keep in mind that the idea is to *not* give your opponent a strong return shot opportunity. It is critical that the ball takes its second floor bounce deep in the backcourt and, preferably, in the vicinity of a corner. This will not allow your opponent to get behind the ball, set up for a return, and hit an aggressive offensive shot. Once a defensive shot is used in a rally, experienced players will frequently hit consecutive defensive shots. This may continue until one player makes a mistake in placement or becomes impatient with the slower, controlled game dictated by defensive shots and aggressively tries to hit a winning shot from a poor contact point. In the latter case, the aggressor usually either wins the rally with his or her shot or sets up the opponent to hit the winner.

We will cover two types of basic defensive shots: the **ceiling shot** and the **around-the-wall ball** shot. Each can be very effective if executed properly and used in the appropriate situation on the court.

Figure 3.31
Corner and pinch kill drill court positions.

ceiling shot
around-the-wall ball

Ceiling Shots

The ceiling shot is the most frequently used defensive shot in racquetball. It is executed by hitting the ball to a point on the ceiling within 3 to 6 feet of the front wall, with the ball rebounding to the front wall, dropping down to the floor, then taking a high arc bounce to the base of the back wall (see figure 3.32). The shot should be angled to finish in one of the back corners without allowing a back wall rebound opportunity. On any ceiling shot, the ball must be hit with sufficient power to drive the ball to the proper location on the ceiling, with the shot finishing deep in the court, close to the base of the back wall. Ceiling shots may be hit with a forehand or a backhand stroke, or with an overhead stroke. The forehand and backhand strokes are executed using the proper fundamentals of each stroke. The only differences in a forehand or backhand ceiling shot are that the contact point is moved forward of the original point approximately 6 to 12 inches, and the angle of the racket face is turned upward to drive the ball into the ceiling on contact with the ball (see figures 3.33a and 3.33b). On the overhead shots, the contact point is slightly behind the normal contact point, and the racket face is also turned upward to direct the ball at the proper angle to the ceiling (see figure 3.33c).

The most common errors made when hitting ceiling shots are (1) too much power, (2) not enough power, and (3) improper angle selection. The first error results in the ball rebounding off the back wall, allowing a strong return. The second error results in the ball dropping far short of the back wall, once again allowing for the possibility of a strong return. The third error usually causes the ball to hit a sidewall improperly on the way to the backcourt, slowing the momentum of the ball and causing it to drop far short of the back wall. Again, this allows a strong return opportunity.

Ceiling shots are most frequently used when a strong offensive return shot is not possible or to force an opponent who is controlling center court to move out of that area and chase the ball into a back corner for the next return. A well-placed ceiling shot will frequently be followed by another ceiling shot because there is very little opportunity to attempt an offensive return to end the rally. An aggressive player may attack a ceiling shot when it first strikes the floor, but the unpredictable timing and bounce of the ball make this a low percentage return. Most often, the re-

Figure 3.32
Ceiling shot.

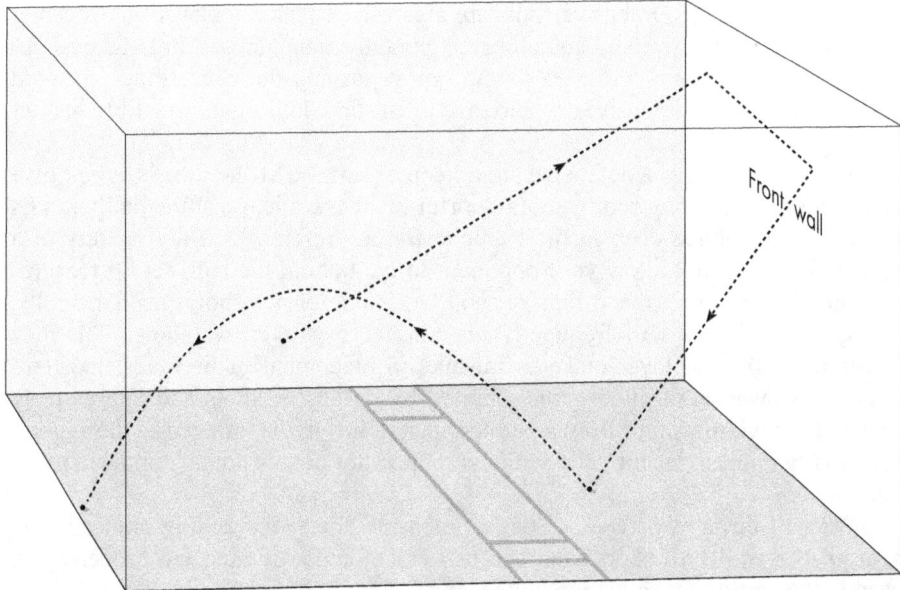

turn of a ceiling ball will be another overhead stroke ceiling shot from deep in the court and will continue the rally. Hitting to your opponent's backhand corner is considered good strategy in most situations because players, especially beginners, usually have a weaker return shot with their backhand than with their forehand strokes.

There are two types of ceiling shots: the down-the-wall ceiling shot and the crosscourt ceiling shot.

Down-the-wall Ceiling Shot

The down-the-wall ceiling shot is also known as the wallpaper or down-the-line ceiling shot. It consists of hitting the ball, from either side of the court, at an angle on the ceiling that will cause the rebound to travel close to and parallel with the near sidewall as it travels into the backcourt area (see figure 3.19a). It should be hit with enough power to drop the second bounce close to the base of the back wall (see figure 3.32). Do not hit into the sidewall, except deep into the back corners, or the ball will drop short of the back wall and set up a strong return opportunity.

A forehand stroke should be used to hit the ball from a low contact point down the forehand sidewall, and a backhand should be used to hit the ball from a low contact point down the backhand sidewall. An overhead stroke may be used to hit a high ball down either sidewall.

Crosscourt Ceiling Shot

The only difference between the crosscourt ceiling shot and the down-the-wall ceiling shot is the ball placement, from right to left, on the ceiling. By hitting the ball at the proper crosscourt angle to the ceiling, the ball will rebound into the opposite back corner of the court instead of staying close to the near sidewall (see figure 3.20a). All other aspects of the shot are the same.

Around-the-wall Ball

The around-the-wall ball should be used sparingly, but if offers a change-up to the ceiling ball as a defensive weapon. The desired result is the same as with other defensive shots: forcing the opponent to move into a backcourt corner to retrieve the ball where a strong offensive return shot would be difficult. It is executed by hitting the ball to a point high on the sidewall within 4 to 6 feet of the ceiling and close to the front wall. The ball will continue on a high path to the front wall, rebound to the opposite sidewall, drop to the floor, and rebound deep into the back corner or near the back wall for the second bounce (see figure 3.34). This shot can be hit to either sidewall but would generally have better results if played to rebound to the backhand corner of the opponent.

The same strokes will be used for the around-the-wall ball as for the ceiling shots: forehand, backhand, and overhead. The racket face will need to be turned at the proper angle to hit the ball to the aiming point when executing the shot.

The most common errors made when hitting around-the-wall balls are (1) hitting with too much power, (2) not hitting with

Figure 3.33
Contact points for ceiling shots.

a Forehand

b Backhand

c Overhead

Figure 3.34
Around-the-wall ball.

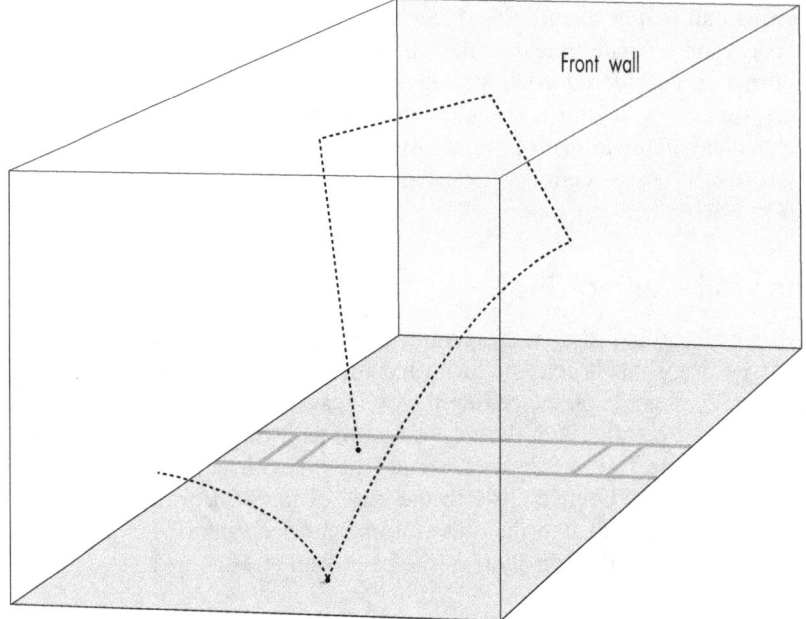

enough power, and (3) not hitting the correct spot on the first sidewall contact. The first error results in the ball rebounding off the back wall, allowing a strong return. The second error results in the ball dropping too short of the back wall, allowing a strong return. The third error usually occurs when the ball is aimed too high and hits the ceiling during the shot. When this happens, the ball loses its momentum and drops into the center court area, resulting in a setup for a strong offensive return.

Table 3.9 lists the fundamentals of basic defensive shots, as well as common errors.

TABLE 3.9	Basic Defensive Shot Summary
CEILING SHOT	**ERRORS**
1. Hit with power.	1. Hitting too soft or too hard.
2. Hit ceiling first.	2. Hitting front wall first.
3. Plan for second bounce in back corner.	3. Allowing second bounce in open court.
4. Don't hit sidewalls (except for deep in backcourt).	4. Hitting sidewalls too soon.
5. Take over center court.	5. Not moving into center court.
AROUND-THE-WALL BALL	**ERRORS**
1. Hit with power.	1. Hitting too soft or too hard.
2. Hit to proper point high on sidewall.	2. Placing shots erratically.
3. Plan for second bounce deep in backcourt or corner.	3. Allowing second bounce in open court.
4. Take over center court.	4. Not moving into center court.

Basic Defensive Shot Drills

Down-the-wall Ceiling Shot Drill: Use forehand, backhand, and overhead strokes.

1. Begin deep in the court, on the right side for forehand ceiling shots and the left side for backhand ceiling shots. Hit overhead ceiling shots from either side of the court.
2. Using good stroke technique, drop the ball and hit a down-the-wall ceiling shot, attempting to keep the ball between you and the sidewall. Use a high bounce for the overhead strokes.
3. Move to the appropriate position and as the rebound comes toward the back wall, hit another down-the-wall ceiling shot. Continue this individual rally as long as you can keep hitting ceiling shots. Count the number of consecutive ceiling shots you can hit without an offensive setup occurring. Compare your scores against yourself for improvement (see figure 3.35a).
4. With two or three players in the court, repeat the drill with players alternating hitting down-the-wall ceiling shots until one player has an offensive setup (see figure 3.35b). When an offensive opportunity presents itself, go for the shot, and then start the drill again.
5. With four or more players in the court, repeat the drill and rotate, hitting down-the-wall ceiling shots, according to the order illustrated in figure 3.35c. This can also be used for conditioning purposes.

Figure 3.35
Down-the-wall ceiling shot drills.

a   One player   b   Two or three players   c   Four players

Crosscourt Ceiling Shot Drill: Use forehand, backhand, and overhead strokes.

1. Begin behind the short line, attempting the crosscourt ceiling shot from various locations using forehand, backhand, and overhead strokes.
2. Arc the ball to the front wall with a hand toss or a light hit with the racket, causing the rebound to set up a ceiling shot attempt. This could be a high bounce for an overhead stroke or lower for a forehand or backhand stroke.
3. Using good stroke technique, hit he rebound for a crosscourt ceiling shot (see figure 3.36a). Observe the location of the second bounce on the floor to determine if the shot would have allowed a strong offensive return. Hit from various court positions and to both back corners. Repeat ten times and compare the number of successful attempts against yourself for improvement.
4. With two players on the court, alternate hitting crosscourt ceiling shots to each other, with one player on the right side of the court using forehand and overhead strokes and the other player on the left side using backhand and overhead strokes (see figure 3.36b). When an offensive opportunity presents itself, go for the shot, and then start the drill again.
5. With more than two players on the court, a clockwise (or counterclockwise) rotation could be used with each player hitting crosscourt ceiling shots from each corner as illustrated in figure 3.36c.

Figure 3.36

Crosscourt ceiling shot drills.

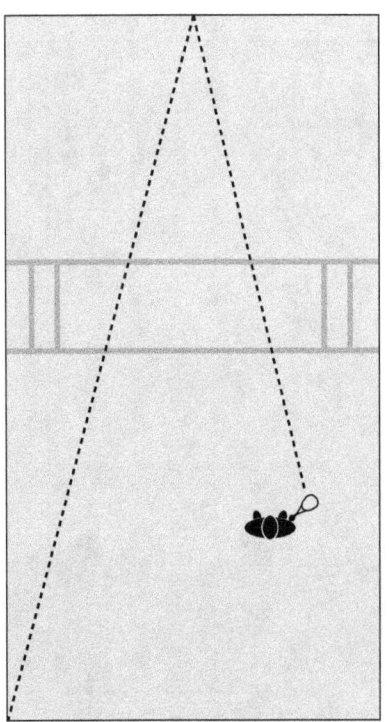
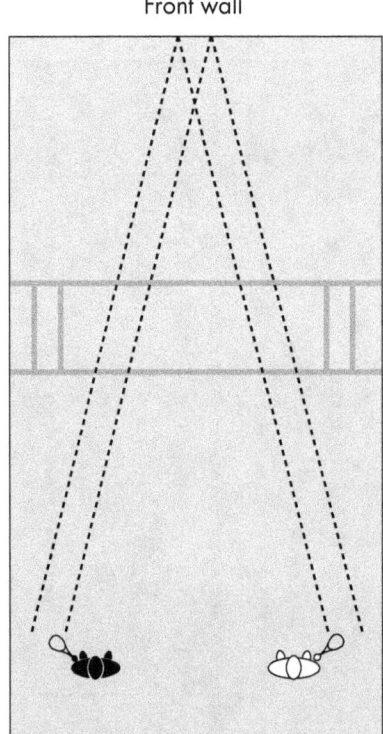
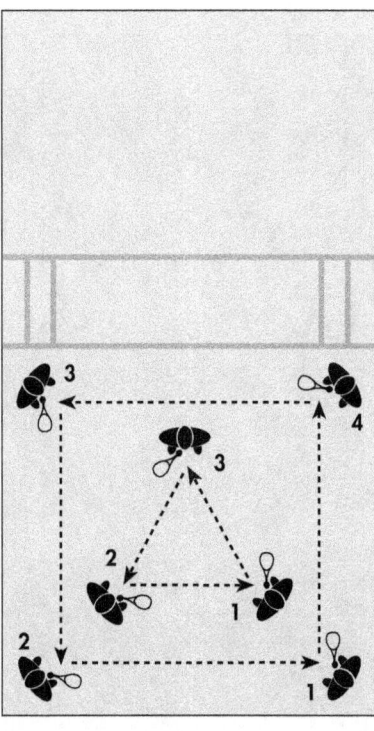

a One player (from either side)

b Two players (hit to each other)

c Three or four player rotation

Ceiling Shot Drill Game for Two Players

The down-the-wall ceiling shot drill and the crosscourt ceiling shot drill can both be executed as a practice game for two players. Execute the drill as outlined in the instructions. Players alternate hitting the first ceiling shot in each rally. Points are scored when a ceiling shot attempt results in a setup for an offensive return. If Player A hits a ceiling shot that causes an offensive setup, score one point for Player B for the occurrence of the setup. Player B can score an additional point for an offensive return shot that cannot be returned by Player A. If the offensive attempt is returned by Player A, Player A scores one point, the rally ends, and a new ceiling shot rally begins. Players must use ceiling shots unless a good offensive opportunity occurs. In the crosscourt ceiling shot drill game, the player hitting first in each rally should hit from the right side of the court.

Around-the-wall Ball Drill: Use forehand and overhead strokes.

1. Begin behind the short line and on the right side of the court.
2. Using good stroke technique, drop the ball, or toss to yourself off the front wall, and hit a forehand or overhead stroke to the sidewall in the upper left front corner area to execute an around-the-wall ball. Use a high bounce setup for the overhead stroke. Hit primarily forehand or overhead strokes to the upper left front corner with this shot, causing the ball to rebound into the deep left (backhand) corner.
3. Observe the area where the second floor bounce occurs, and adjust the shot angle, if necessary, to have the ball "die" (second bounce) in the back corner/back wall area. Repeat the shot with any adjustments.
4. Do not spend a great deal of practice time on this shot, but repeat this drill occasionally to refresh your angles and desired results for an around-the-wall ball.

SKILL 4 — Playing Off the Back Wall

The ability to play the ball off the back wall is vital to being a well-rounded racquetball player. A skilled player can often hit a strong offensive return from a back wall rebound. To do this, the player must correctly anticipate the force and direction of the rebound and move into the proper position for the return shot. Most back wall rebound returns will be made with a basic forehand or backhand stroke, and a variety of kill shots or passing shots can be executed on these returns.

In order to allow the ball to travel to, and rebound off, the back wall, a player must develop the judgment and patience not to swing at every ball coming off the front wall. Rather, the player must judge the speed and angle of the ball and quickly determine if it has the direction and velocity to create a back wall rebound opportunity. If the shot does not have the capability of a back wall rebound, the player must decide to hit the ball as it is coming off the front wall. If it will create a rebound opportunity, the player should allow the ball to travel past his or her body, and move to the proper court location to hit the back wall rebound.

CUE: Use every possible back wall rebound to hit a strong offensive return.

Two important techniques should be used whenever playing a back wall rebound. Players should never lose eye contact with the ball as it passes them to the back wall, and they should always keep their feet moving to allow split-second adjustments in court position as the ball rebounds off the back wall.

The most common errors made when hitting back wall rebound shots are (1) improper court position for the stroke or contact point, (2) poor stroke fundamentals, and (3) indecision on which shot to hit with the stroke. The first error, improper court position for the stroke or contact point, causes erratic hitting, with the ball often going down to the floor or into a sidewall. It can also cause players to jam their stroke arm into their body by positioning too close to the ball or to miss the ball completely by being too far away to make contact with the ball. One other result from the first error can be contacting the ball too high, which may give the opponent a setup on his or her next shot. The second error, poor stroke fundamentals, often is a side effect of the first error. It can also be caused by lack of confidence in playing off the back wall. The result could be weak return shots or lack of control in the placement of the return shots. The third error, indecision on which return shot to hit, often results in choppy strokes and late swings, causing the ball to be hit to the floor or a sidewall.

CUE: Get behind the contact point and keep your feet moving forward with the ball as it comes to you off the back wall.

There are three basic ways that a ball coming off the back wall can be played: on the fly, after the bounce, and out of a corner. One other use of the back wall is in a desperation situation, when the ball is actually directed into the back wall, with the hope that it will travel to the front wall before it hits the floor.

Back Wall Rebound on the Fly

The most frequent use of the back wall rebound shot is after the ball, coming from the front wall, has bounced off the floor, struck the back wall, is now on the fly (in the air), and must be played before striking the floor again (see figure 3.37a). In order to execute a proper return, the player must anticipate the angle and power of the ball and move into position to execute the forehand or backhand stroke fundamentals. Because it has already contacted the floor once, this rebound will have lost some of its velocity and will usually have to be played in the back half of the court.

CUE: If the ball bounces on the floor before hitting the back wall, move toward the back wall.

Often, it must be played close to the back wall. It is helpful if the player moves to a location slightly closer to the back wall than the anticipated contact point and then shuffles his or her feet to the stroke position as the ball comes off the back wall. Balls rebounding between the player and the right sidewall should be hit with a forehand stroke, while balls rebounding between the player and the left sidewall should be hit with a backhand stroke.

When using a forehand stroke, the ball should ideally be contacted at or below knee height and directly between the left knee and the sidewall. On a backhand stroke, the ball should be contacted at or below knee height and 6 to 12 inches in front of the right knee. On both strokes, the elbow and wrist should be fully extended at the point of contact with the ball. Because the ball is moving in the same direction as the stroke, the downswing motion must start sooner than when hitting a ball coming at the player from the front wall. Practice will allow the player to adjust the timing on this shot.

Back Wall Rebound After the Bounce

This back wall rebound opportunity happens less frequently than the rebound on the fly. It occurs when the ball has been hit hard and/or high to the front wall and travels to the back wall without striking the floor. The ball will still have a great deal of momentum as it rebounds off the back wall and will drop to the floor (first

Figure 3.37
Back wall rebound.

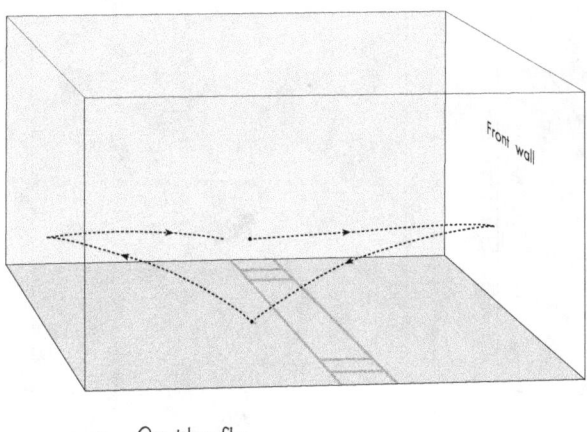

a On the fly

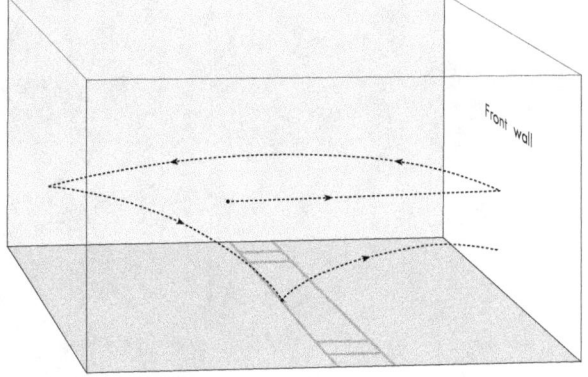

b On the bounce

bounce) and continue far into the frontcourt area, where the second floor bounce will occur (see figure 3.37b). Players must anticipate the ball hitting the back wall before striking the floor, and immediately begin moving to the frontcourt area to be in position for their return shot.

CUE: If the ball is going to hit the back wall without hitting the floor first, move toward the frontcourt.

Basic forehand or backhand strokes may be used. The frontcourt location for these returns also allows the player to choose from a wide variety of shots, depending on the location of the contact point in relationship to the opponent's court position. This return shot will often be hit while on the run, moving with the ball as it rebounds toward the front wall, and it can still be played coming off the front wall a second time if it has enough momentum to carry it that far.

The same stroke fundamentals should be used here as in the rebound on the fly, except when moving to keep up with the ball, the footwork may need to be improvised "on the run." Soft corner kills and passing shots are the most frequently used returns for back wall rebounds after the bounce.

Back Wall Rebound from a Corner

There will be occasions when a ball will travel diagonally across the court, bounce on the floor, hit the sidewall, and rebound off the back wall (see figure 3.38a). Following a similar path, this shot may also hit the back wall first and then rebound off the sidewall (see figure 3.38b). Anticipating which way the ball will go into, and come out of, the corner is important to getting into proper position for the return shot.

CUE: Reading the correct angle the ball will come out of the back corners is essential for a good return.

Most players will hit a defensive return because of the difficulty of getting behind the ball on a corner rebound and preparing for an offensive stroke. The ceiling shot is frequently used to return a tough corner rebound. If the player is prepared for an offensive return, and the rebound sets up an offensive opportunity, the player should hit the best shot possible that may end the rally.

Figure 3.38

Corner/back wall rebound.

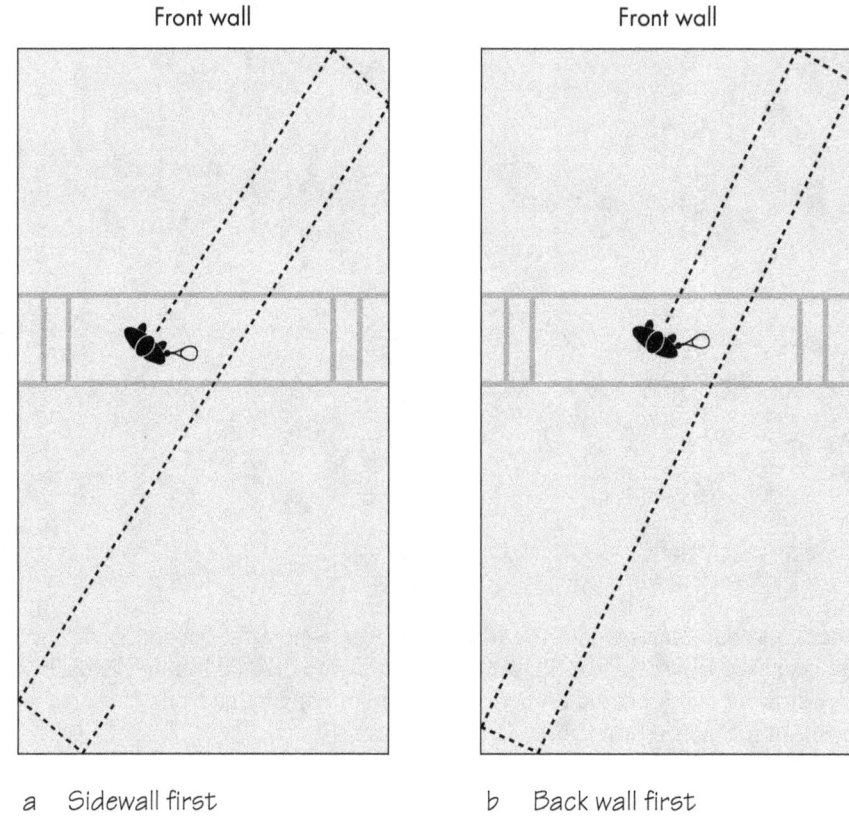

a Sidewall first   b Back wall first

CUE: Keep the ball in your vision at all times when attempting these returns.

Cutting the ball off (hitting it) before it goes into the back corner is also a good alternative, if the player can make a reasonable return. This could be either an offensive or defensive return, but not a desperation stab at the ball. Hitting the ball before it reaches the back corner will eliminate the difficulty of playing the corner rebound shot. Experience and good judgment will help players decide whether it would be better to cut off the ball or play the back wall rebound from the corner.

A back wall/sidewall rebound from a corner will cause different problems than a sidewall/back wall rebound. The back wall/sidewall shot will usually stay on one side of the player's body, allowing the player to keep an eye on the ball throughout the path of the ball (see figure 3.39a). It will rebound to a racket contact point closer to the sidewall and toward the short line, forcing the player to move quickly into this area once the ball has gone into the corner. This return should be hit with a backhand stroke if it is in the left corner and with a forehand stroke if it is in the right corner.

The sidewall/back wall shot, on the other hand, can force the player to make a complete pivot before the return stroke in order to keep an eye on the ball. For this reason, it is sometimes referred to as a wraparound ball or a wraparound shot. This ball will rebound to a racket contact point much closer to the back wall and to the center court position than the back wall/sidewall rebound (see figure 3.39b). An experienced player, anticipating the different angle of this rebound, will move toward the opposite sidewall, keeping the ball in full front view throughout the corner rebound (see figure 3.40a). If the ball is not moving too swiftly, some players prefer to make a complete pivot and stroke the ball as it passes the other side of their body (see figure 3.40b).

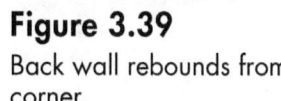

Figure 3.39
Back wall rebounds from corner.

a   Back wall/sidewall

b   Sidewall/back wall

Figure 3.40
Sidewall/back wall corner rebounds.

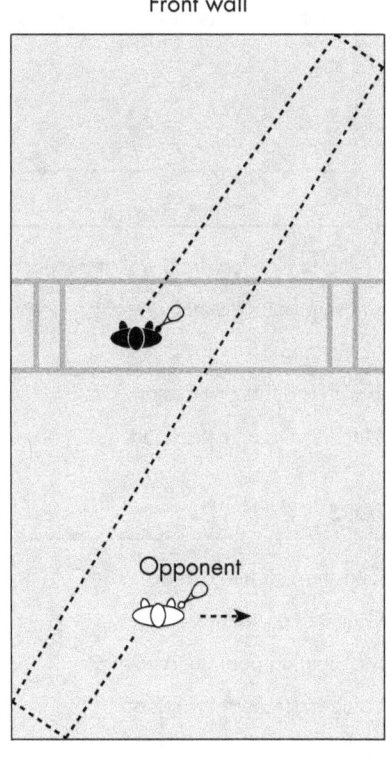
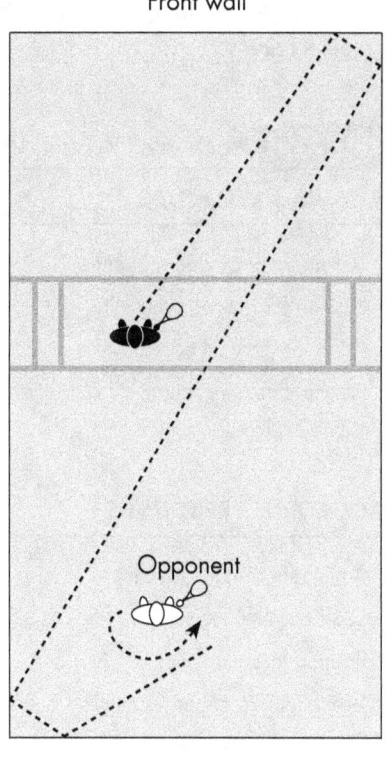

a   Move to opposite sidewall

b   Pivot with ball

The key to playing this return correctly is to anticipate which wall the ball will hit first, decide where the ball will carom off the wall, and then move quickly to the appropriate position to hit the desired return shot. Observing corner rebounds and practicing these returns will greatly enhance your ability to play the ball on back wall rebounds from a corner.

Table 3.10 lists the fundamentals of back wall rebounds, as well as common errors.

Back Wall Rebound Drills

Back Wall Rebound on the Fly Drill: Use forehand and backhand strokes.

1. Begin at the receiving line.
2. At **midcourt** (the area of the court between the service line and the receiving line), face the right sidewall. Drop the ball and hit a solid forehand stroke to the front wall. Direct the ball to the right side of the court, with enough power and height to result in a backcourt bounce and then a back wall rebound (see figure 3.41).
3. Move into position to hit a forehand stroke as the ball rebounds on the fly from the back wall.
4. Before the ball drops to the floor off the back wall, use good forehand stroke fundamentals to drive the ball on a low, flat line to the front wall.
5. Repeat this drill facing the left sidewall for the backhand stroke. Drive the setup stroke (#2 above) down the left side of the court, and follow instructions in #3 and #4, adjusting for a backhand stroke.
6. Practice both the forehand and the backhand back wall rebound returns until you are able to hit at least 9 out of 10 returns to the front wall with some power and accuracy.

TABLE 3.10 Back Wall Rebound Summary

BACK WALL REBOUNDS	ERRORS
1. Anticipate back wall rebound.	1. Trying to hit every front wall rebound.
2. Position for proper stroke.	2. Chasing ball—not being ready.
3. Hit at low contact point.	3. Contacting the ball too high.
4. Attempt offensive return.	4. Using no strategy on return.
5. Take over center court.	5. Not moving to center court.

BACK CORNER REBOUNDS	ERRORS
1. Anticipate corner rebound.	1. Chasing ball into corner.
2. Read angle of rebound.	2. Guessing on rebound angle.
3. Position for return shot.	3. Maintaining poor court position.
4. Use defensive return (usually).	4. Using no strategy on return.
5. Take over center court.	5. Not moving to center court.

midcourt

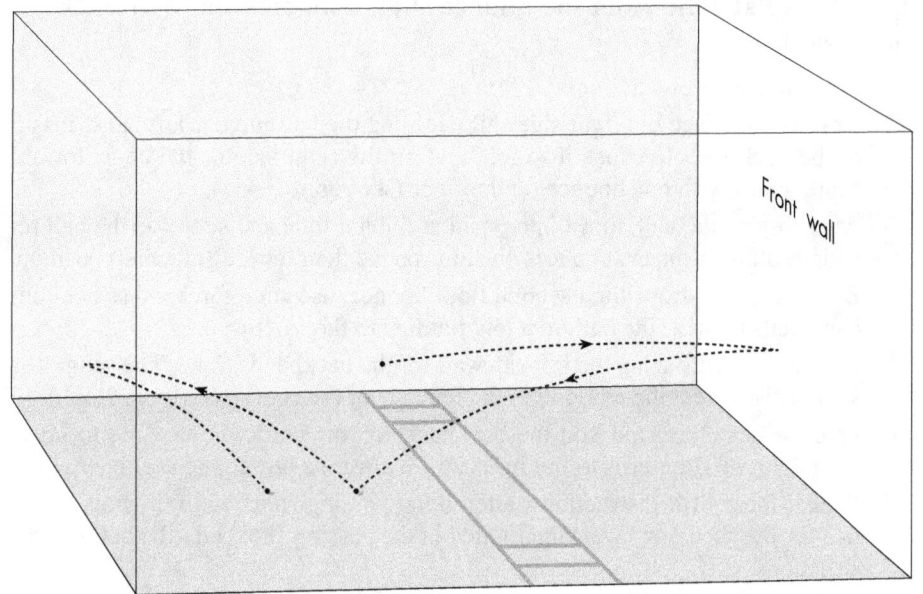

Figure 3.41
Back wall rebounds on the fly drill with one player.

7. Repeat these drill instructions, attempting passing shots and kill shots. Practice for the accuracy levels mentioned in the passing shot and kill shot drill instructions.
8. With two players in the court, the second player may toss or hit the ball to set up the back wall rebound opportunities, as in #2 above. The ball may be set up off the front wall or it may be played directly into the back wall area for the drill (see figures 3.42a and 3.42b).

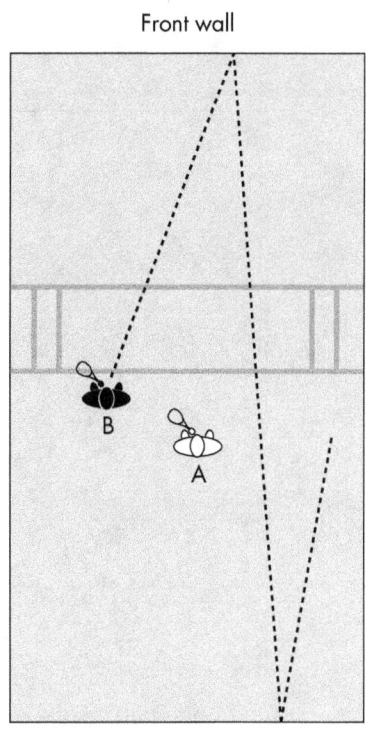
a   Off front wall

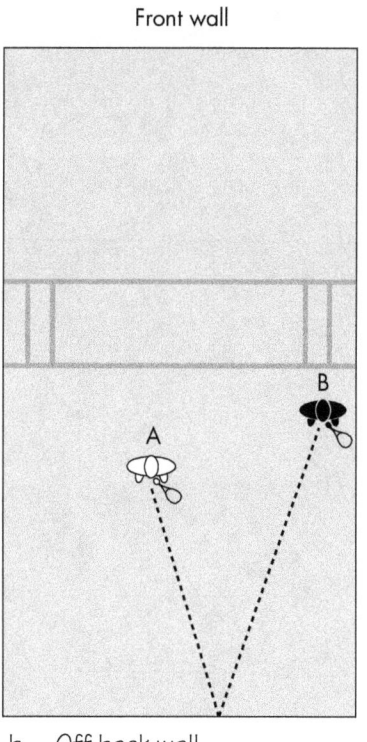
b   Off back wall

Figure 3.42
Back wall rebounds on the fly drill with partner.

Back Wall Rebound After the Bounce Drill: Use forehand and backhand strokes.

1. Begin at the receiving line.
2. At midcourt, face the right sidewall. Holding the ball in your left hand, toss it to the back wall to cause it to rebound on the right side of the court toward center court with one bounce on the floor (see figure 3.43a).
3. After tossing the ball, move into position to hit a forehand stroke as the ball rebounds off the wall and bounces one time on the floor toward your court position.
4. Before the ball drops for a second floor bounce, use good forehand stroke fundamentals to drive the ball on a low flat line to the front wall.
5. Repeat this drill facing the left sidewall for the backhand stroke. The setup toss should also direct the rebound to the left side of the court (see figure 3.43b).
6. Practice both forehand and the backhand returns until you are able to hit at least 9 out of 10 returns to the front wall with some power and accuracy.
7. Repeat these drill instructions, attempting passing shots and kill shots. Practice for the accuracy levels mentioned in the passing shot and kill shot drill instructions.
8. With two players on the court, the second player may toss or hit the ball to set up the back wall rebound opportunities (see figure 3.42).

Back Wall Rebound from a Corner Drill: Use forehand and backhand strokes.

1. Begin in the center court position.
2. Face the right sidewall (slightly angle to back corner).
3. Holding the ball in your left hand, toss the ball to the back right corner, striking sidewall/back wall on the first toss. Use the opposite order for the next toss, and alternate as needed for practice (see figures 3.44a and 3.44b).

Figure 3.43
Back wall rebound drill.

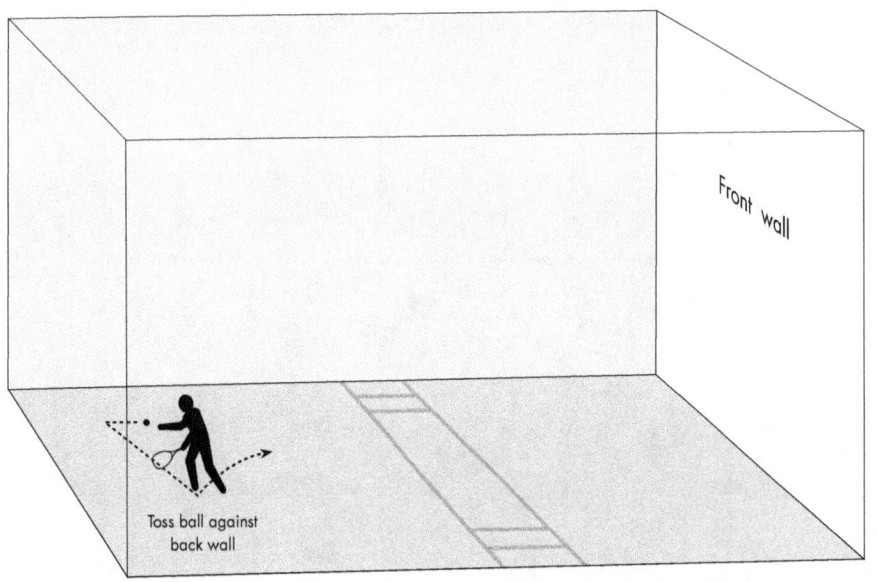

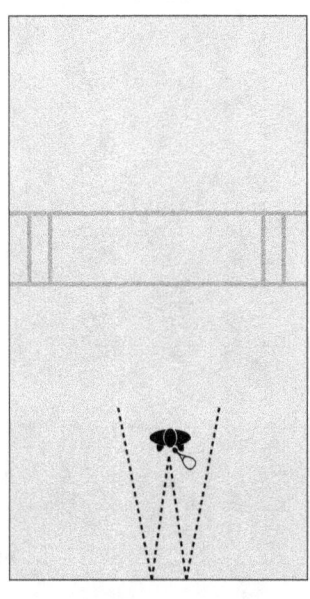

a   b   Toss ball to rebound for forehand or backhand stroke

Figure 3.44
Corner rebound drill: Toss into corner.

4. After tossing the ball, move into position to hit a forehand stroke as the ball rebounds out of the corner and bounces one time on the floor toward your court position.
5. Using good forehand stroke fundamentals, hit offensive shots or defensive shots, depending on the opportunity presented by the corner rebound.
6. Repeat this drill facing the left sidewall and tossing the ball into the back left corner.
7. Evaluate your results, with a target of at least 6 out of 10 returns not allowing an offensive setup for your opponent's next shot.
8. With two players on the court, have the second player toss or hit the ball into the corner, creating rebounds to be played either on the fly or with a bounce after the corner rebound (see figure 3.45). Alternate between hitting into the sidewall first and the back wall first. (Use safety precautions for second player's court position when hitting the ball toward his or her position.)

Desperation Back Wall Shots (Hitting into the back wall)

The name, desperation back wall shots, refers to any return hit directly into the back wall. There are only two situations when a ball should be hit directly into the back wall: (1) when a passing shot has gone by your position into backcourt and (2) when a ball is dropping so close to the back wall that you cannot get behind the ball for a forward stroke. These are considered desperate situations and the name, desperation back wall shot, should remind you that these are the only ap-

Figure 3.45
Corner rebound drill: Two players.

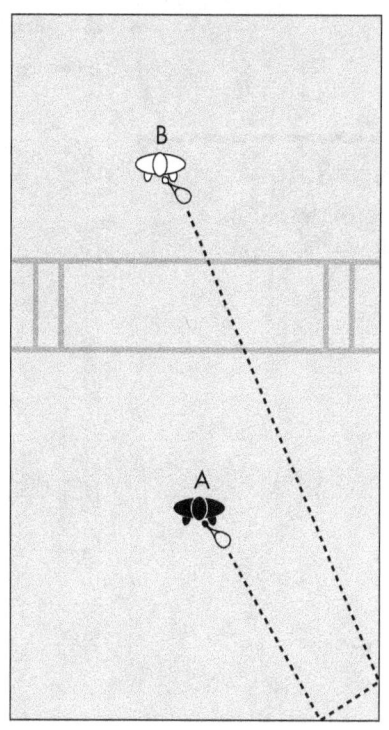

propriate times to use this return. Any other time the ball is hit into the back wall, it is the result of poor strategy or laziness. Many beginning players have the temptation to hit the ball into the back wall when caught out of position or not prepared to hit a proper stroke to the front wall. This type of return often results in an offensive setup for your opponent.

When hitting this shot, the ball must be driven with power into the back wall at an upward angle to allow the ball to go past your body and arc to the front wall (see figure 3.46). This almost always results in an easy return opportunity for your opponent and, consequently, should be used sparingly and only in desperation situations. A good strategy to use with a desperation back wall shot is to attempt to hit a high **lob** (a ball hit high and soft to the front wall, rebounding and bouncing with a high arc into the backcourt) or a ceiling shot, forcing your opponent to play the return shot deep in the court, preferably to the backhand side. A forehand stroke should be used when the ball is on the left side of the court, and a backhand stroke should be used when the ball is on the right side of the court. Pivot to face the sidewall where the ball is located, and hit the appropriate stroke. When close to the back wall, you must use a short, swift stroke with very little follow-through, attempting to hit the ball into the back wall without having it rebound back into your racket. You may also have to lean or duck under the ball to avoid being hit in the face or head on the rebound. Return to center court position and hope for another opportunity in the rally.

Table 3.11 lists the fundamentals of desperation back wall shots, as well as common errors.

lob

TABLE 3.11 Desperation Back Wall Shots Summary	
PASSING SHOTS AT MIDCOURT	**ERRORS**
1. Pivot to face sidewall.	1. Reaching across body/no pivot.
2. Determine ball is past you, but reachable.	2. Giving up on return.
3. Stroke at ball with upward swing.	3. Not swinging; hitting to sidewall.
4. Return to center court.	4. Not moving to center court.

Figure 3.46

Angle of desperation back wall shot.

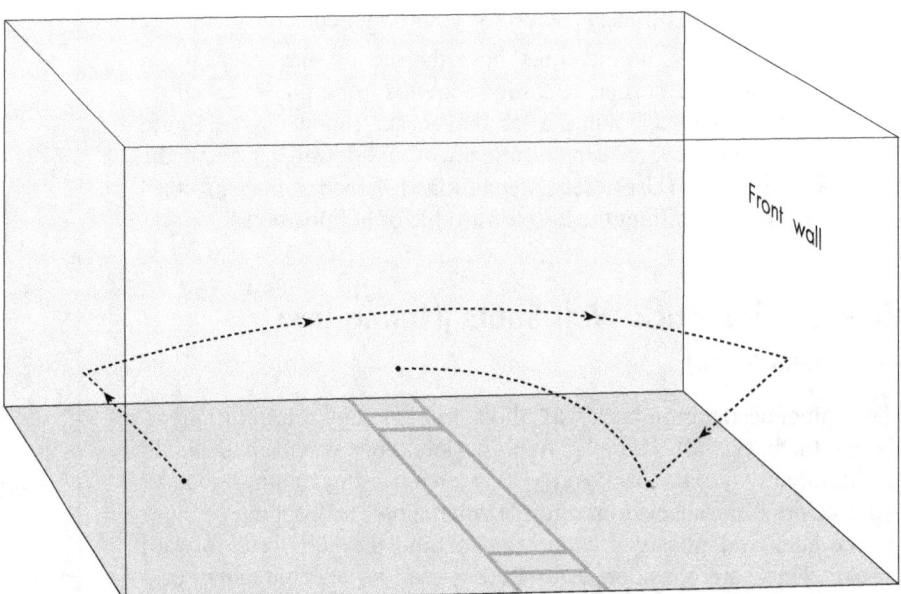

Desperation Back Wall Shot Drills

Desperation Return Off Passing Shot: Use forehand and backhand strokes.

1. Begin at receiving line.
2. At midcourt, face the right sidewall. Raise the racket on a backswing for a backhand stroke. Drop the ball off the right foot, toward the back wall.
3. Step toward the ball and hit it, with a backhand stroke, into the back wall. Use an upward swing to lift the ball, causing it to arc to the front wall as it rebounds off the back wall (see figures 3.47a and 3.47b).
4. Repeat steps #2 and #3, facing the left sidewall and using a forehand stroke.
5. Repeat from various midcourt positions, attempting to return the ball to the front wall while not allowing a strong offensive return opportunity for your opponent.

Desperation Return Close to Back Wall Drill: Use forehand and backhand strokes.

1. Begin 3 feet from back wall, away from sidewalls.
2. Face the left sidewall. Raise the racket in the backswing for a forehand stroke. With the ball in the left hand, extend the left arm toward the sidewall and toss the ball head high.
3. As the ball returns to chest level, use a forehand stroke to drive the ball upward into the back wall, causing it to arc to the front wall as it rebounds off the back wall (see figure 3.48).
4. Repeat steps #2 and #3, facing the right sidewall and using a backhand stroke.
5. Repeat from various back wall positions, attempting to return the ball to the front wall while not allowing a strong offensive return opportunity for your opponent.

Figure 3.47

Desperation back wall drill.

a Back wall overhead angle   b Side angle

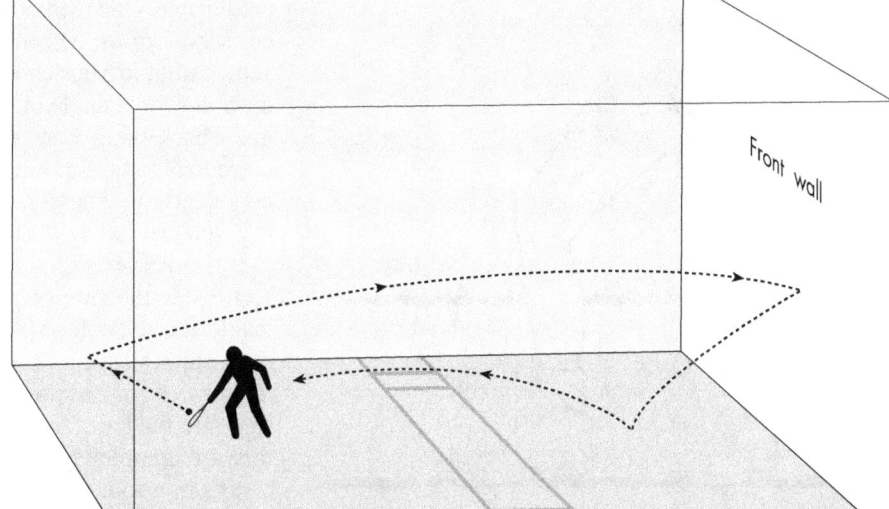

Figure 3.48
Desperation return close to back wall drill.

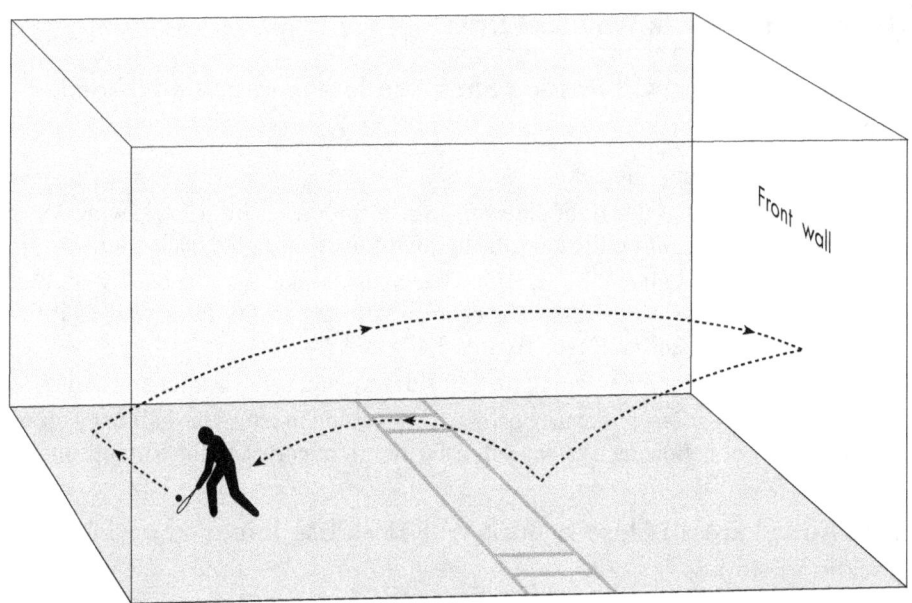

SKILL 5 — Serve and Return of Serve

The serve is the single most important aspect of the game of racquetball. Every rally begins with a serve, and points can be scored only by the player serving. The serve often determines how the remainder of the rally will be played, depending on the type of serve and the return produced by the opponent.

The serve is no longer looked upon as merely a method of starting play. It can, and should, be used as a serious offensive weapon. An aggressive offensive serve will often produce a weak return by the receiver, possibly resulting in a setup for a rally-ending shot by the server. It may also result in no return at all, called an **ace**.

ace

The serve is the only time in racquetball that you, as a player, have total control over your shot selection and contact point. You may predetermine your strategy by choosing your best shot, and you may place your serve specifically to take advantage of your opponent's weaknesses. As a smart player, you do not want your serve to be predictable. One method for avoiding this is to have different serves from the same general location in the service zone. Align in your chosen spot, and do not become predictable by the angle of your body or your racket position in the backswing. Use variations in your shot selection and placement to take advantage of your strengths and/or your opponent's weaknesses. By doing this while you are serving, you can dictate the tempo and strategy of the rally.

The serve begins with the server positioning both feet inside the service zone. Place both feet touching or inside the short line (see figure 3.49) while facing the right sidewall for a forehand serve. Stand as far back in the service zone as possible, allowing maximum space to step into the ball for more power on the serve. (Stepping forward completely out of the service zone on the serve results in a foot fault.) Raise the right arm and racket in the backswing position and bend the knees to get in the ready position to serve (see figure 3.50). Drop or bounce

Figure 3.49
Both feet on short line.

the ball with the left hand according to the type of serve being used. Hit the ball to the front wall first, and cause it to bounce behind the short line before hitting two sidewalls, the back wall, or the ceiling. After the ball has passed the short line, quickly move back into the center court position to play the next shot.

The most common errors made when serving are (1) failing to think through the shot strategy and placement before starting the serve motion, (2) hitting the ball too high on drive serves, (3) serving the ball into the middle of the court, and (4) failing to move into center court position after the serve passes the short line. The first error, failure to think through the shot strategy and placement, often results in poor selection of serves or predictable serves. It also results in the serve simply starting the rally, instead of being a strong offensive weapon. The second error, hitting the ball too high on drive serves, results in easy returns for the receiver. The third error, serving the ball into the middle of the court, allows easy returns for the receiver and prevents the server from moving directly into the center court position after serving. The fourth error, failure to move into center court position after serving, allows the return of serve to end many rallies with passing shots down the sides of the court and makes many other returns difficult to play.

Figure 3.50
Ready position for serve.

Z serve

There are three basic serves in racquetball: the drive serve, the lob serve, and the **Z serve**. There are many variations available on each of these basic serves, with only slight adjustments necessary.

The following constitute the unwritten rules of the serve:

1. *Always* serve to your opponent's backhand, except as an occasional change-up to keep him or her from overplaying the backhand side of the court while ignoring the forehand area. (If your opponent has a better backhand than forehand return, use good judgment on serve placement.)
2. *Always* have a plan of attack before dropping the ball for the serve.
3. *Always* be unpredictable by frequently changing shot selection and/or shot placement.
4. *Always* move to center court as soon as the serve passes the short line. (Occasionally, shot anticipation will cause you to move to an area other than center court for the next shot. Use center court as much as possible.)
5. *Never* double fault. Make your opponent earn the right to serve.

Drive Serve

The drive serve is the most frequently used serve in racquetball. The drive serve may be hit with a forehand, a backhand, or an overhead stroke. For the forehand and backhand strokes, the ball should be contacted very close to the floor and driven with power on a low, flat line to the front wall (see figure 3.51). For the overhead stroke, the ball must bounce high enough on the drop to allow an overhead contact point, and the ball must be hit with power at the appropriate angles (see figure 3.52). On each of these serves, the racket face must be adjusted to the proper angle at the contact point for different shot placements.

There are three basic drive serves frequently used in racquetball: the back wall/corner drive serve, the sidewall/corner drive serve, and the short sidewall

Figure 3.51
Forehand and backhand drive serve angle.

drive serve, also called a jam serve (see figure 3.53). Each can be very effective, depending on your execution of the serve and the skill of your opponent.

The back wall/corner drive serve causes problems for the receiver in determining how the ball will rebound out of the corner, as was discussed earlier under "Skill 4 Playing off the Back Wall." When hit close to the back wall/sidewall corner, the ball will often rebound parallel to the sidewall, forcing a difficult return of the serve.

The sidewall/corner drive serve causes similar judgment problems for the receiver. A ball hitting the sidewall first will rebound sharply into the deep center court area and force the receiver to move away from the wall to play the shot properly. This change-up between the two shots, especially when the ball angle is difficult to judge going into the corner, creates placement and contact point problems for the receiver.

The short sidewall serve should be hit to rebound directly into the body position of the receiver. This forces the receiver to move out of the path of the ball

Figure 3.52
Overhead drive serve contact point and angle.

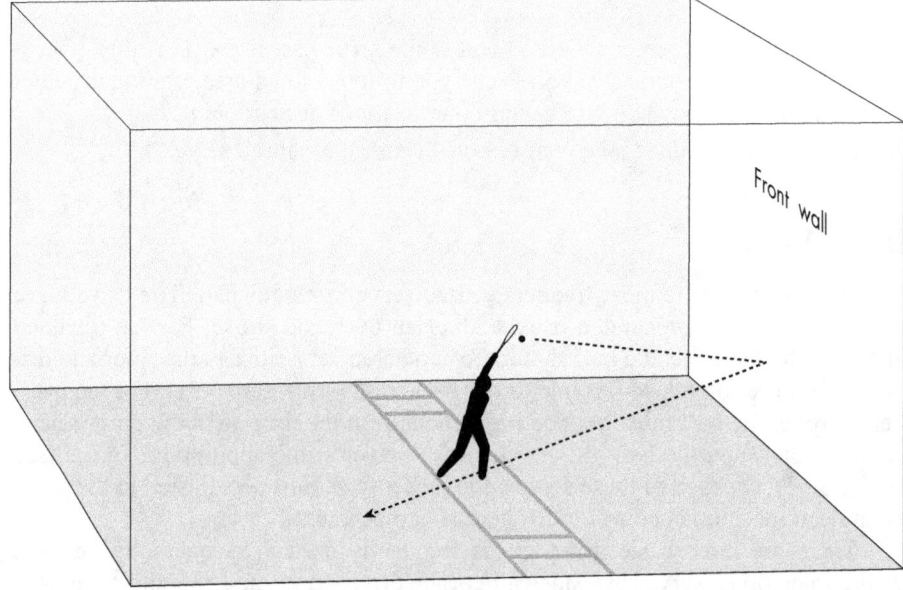

Figure 3.53
Three basic drive serves.

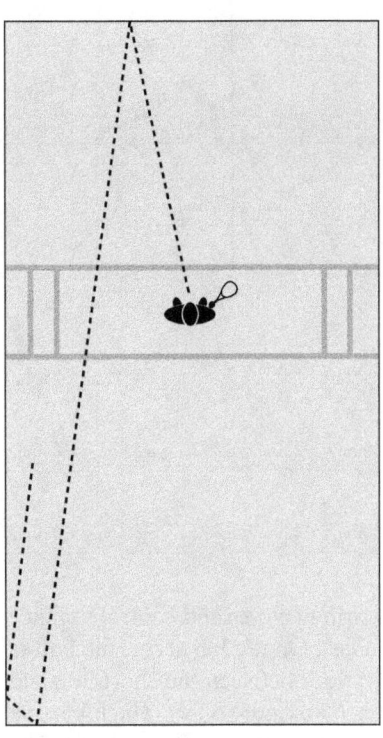 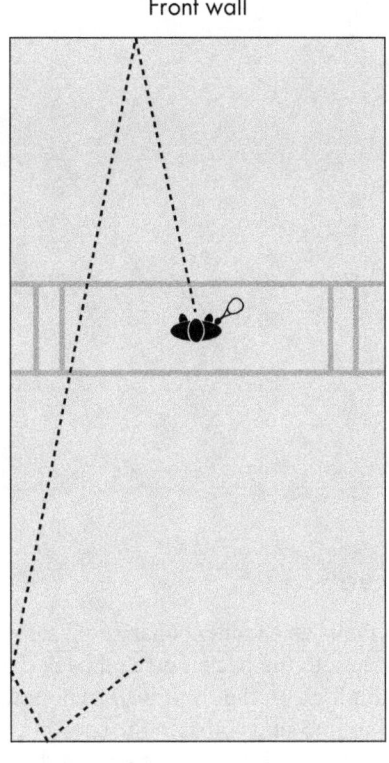 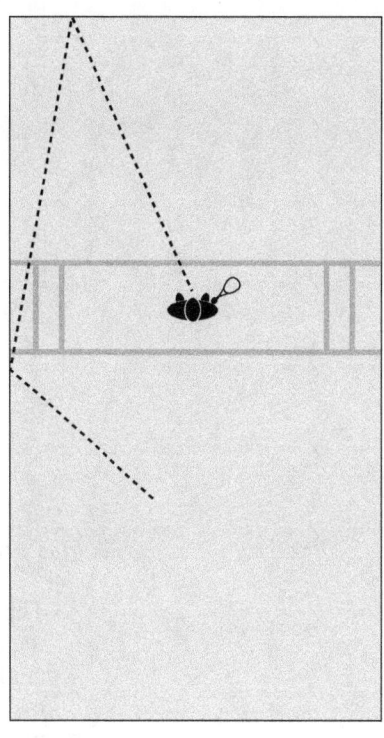

Back wall/corner drive serveSidewall/corner drive serveShort sidewall drive serve

and stroke at the ball at the same time, often resulting in a weak offensive return or a defensive return. When hitting this serve with a forehand or backhand stroke, a player can learn to drive the ball into the sidewall close to the floor. This results in a short hop or a rollout (similar to a kill shot) and is difficult or impossible to return.

Table 3.12 lists the fundamentals of the drive serve, as well as common errors.

TABLE 3.12 Drive Serve Summary

DRIVE SERVE	ERRORS
1. Plan serve strategy.	1. Not developing pre-serve plan of attack.
2. Variety of serves from each spot.	2. Serving predictably by alignment.
3. Begin with feet on short line.	3. Not using all of the service zone to build shot momentum.
4. Contact the ball low.	4. Contacting the ball too high.
5. Hit the ball low and flat.	5. Hitting too high on front wall.
6. Place the ball for a difficult return shot.	6. Placing the ball in an easy setup for offensive return.
7. Move to center court.	7. Not moving to center court.

Figure 3.54
Side view of lob serve.

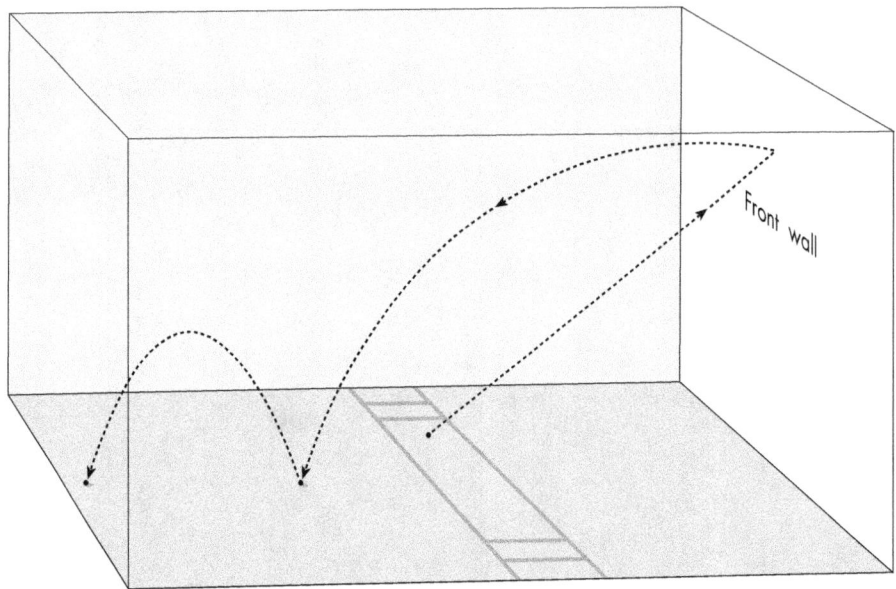

Lob Serve

The lob serve is an excellent change-up serve, requiring finesse and control to place the ball deep into the backcourt and back corner areas. On the lob serve, the ball is angled to hit high on the front wall, rebound to the floor between the short line and the receiving line, and finish in the back corner area (see figure 3.54). The lob serve may be hit as a crosscourt serve or as a down-the-wall serve (see figure 3.55). The

Figure 3.55
Overhead view of lob serve.

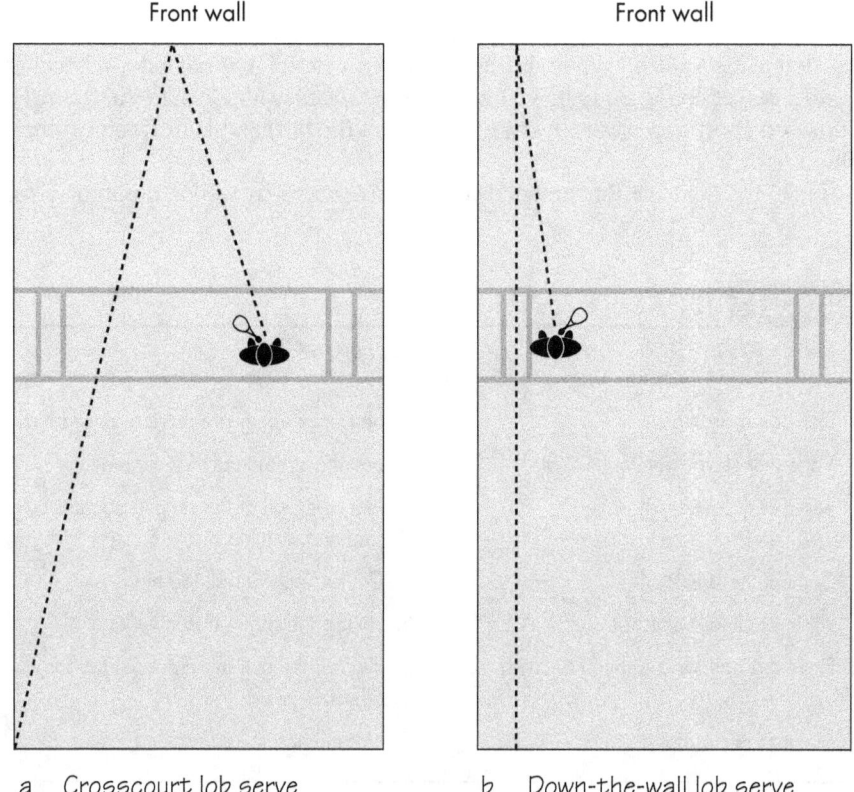

a   Crosscourt lob serve   b   Down-the-wall lob serve

receiver may not attack a serve in front of the receiving line until after the ball has bounced on the floor. This protects the server from the receiver rushing forward and striking the lob serve in front of the receiving line. A well-placed lob serve forces the receiver to hit a defensive shot on the return of serve. The lob serve may be hit with a forehand, a backhand, or an overhead lob stroke.

For the forehand and backhand lob, the ball should be contacted between the knee and hip, and the racket face must be angled toward the upper front wall on contact (see figure 3.56). The ball will be contacted higher and more toward the front wall than in a normal forehand or backhand stroke. The weight should be shifted forward on the stroke, but the elbow and wrist snap must be controlled to provide the amount of power needed to accomplish the lob serve objectives.

For the overhead stroke, the ball should be contacted above the head and a few inches behind the normal contact point (see figure 3.57). Once again, the racket face must be angled toward the upper front wall on contact. The ball must be bounced accurately and hard enough to allow an overhead contact point on the serve. The server should step into the overhead stroke and drive the ball with the amount of power needed to place the ball properly.

The two most common lob serves are the down-the-wall lob serve and the crosscourt lob serve (see figure 3.55). Because the ball moves slowly during a lob serve, it is not critical to use positioning in the service zone to disguise the type of serve being used. Therefore, most players will prefer to serve from the same side of the service zone as they are hitting the down-the-wall lob serve and from the middle or opposite side of the service zone for a crosscourt lob serve. In either case, remember to move back into center court as soon as the ball passes the short line on the serve.

Table 3.13 lists the fundamentals of the lob serve, as well as common errors.

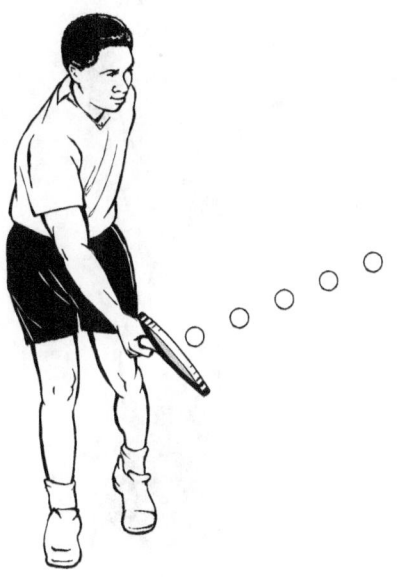

Figure 3.56
Forehand contact point on lob serve.

Half-Lob Serve

The **half-lob serve,** also called the **garbage serve,** is very similar to the lob serve, with one exception. The half-lob serve should be hit to the front wall about head high, to rebound and bounce about shoulder height into the back wall corner (see figure 3.58). If placed accurately, this will not allow the receiver to hit a strong offensive return. All other aspects of this serve, including stroke technique, are comparable to the lob serve.

half-lob serve
garbage serve

TABLE 3.13 Lob Serve Summary

LOB SERVE (ALSO HALF-LOB AND HIGH Z)	ERRORS
1. Plan serve strategy.	1. Not developing pre-serve plan of attack.
2. Align for best serve angles.	2. Not using best serve angles.
3. Use proper power to drop shot deep in back corner.	3. Using too much or too little power.
4. Hit at angle to place ball deep in back corner.	4. Hitting at poor angle, resulting in setup or easy return.
5. Move to center court.	5. Not moving to center court.

Figure 3.57
Overhead contact point on lob serve.

Z Serve

The Z serve utilizes similar principles to the drive serve, also requiring power and accuracy to be effective. To hit a Z serve, the ball is served with a low, powerful forehand stroke to the right front wall, close to the corner. From here the ball will rebound into the sidewall, then angle across the court toward the opposite sidewall. The ball must bounce on the floor behind the short line and before hitting the second sidewall or the back wall to be a legal serve. When the ball bounces off the floor and into the sidewall, the power of the shot will cause the ball to ricochet off the sidewall at an unusual angle, almost parallel to the back wall (see figure 3.59). These sharp crisscrossing angles give this serve its name, the Z serve.

The player hitting a Z serve should align in the middle area of the service zone, similar to the alignment for a drive serve. The serve should almost always be hit to the receiver's backhand, and the Z serve is no exception. Plan to take advantage of the weakest aspect of your opponent's return of serve, which usually is a backhand return from deep in the back corner. When executed properly, the ball will ricochet off the sidewall, parallel with and close to the back wall. This allows the receiver almost no opportunity to get behind the ball to hit a strong offensive return. A weak return, or a defensive return, then puts the server in control of the rally.

It is important for the Z serve to be hit deep into the back corner of the court. If it is hit too shallow along the sidewall, an experienced player will anticipate the angle of the rebound and move into position for the return shot. A midcourt setup will often allow a strong offensive return that may end the rally in favor of the receiver (see figure 3.60).

Figure 3.58
Side view of half-lob serve.

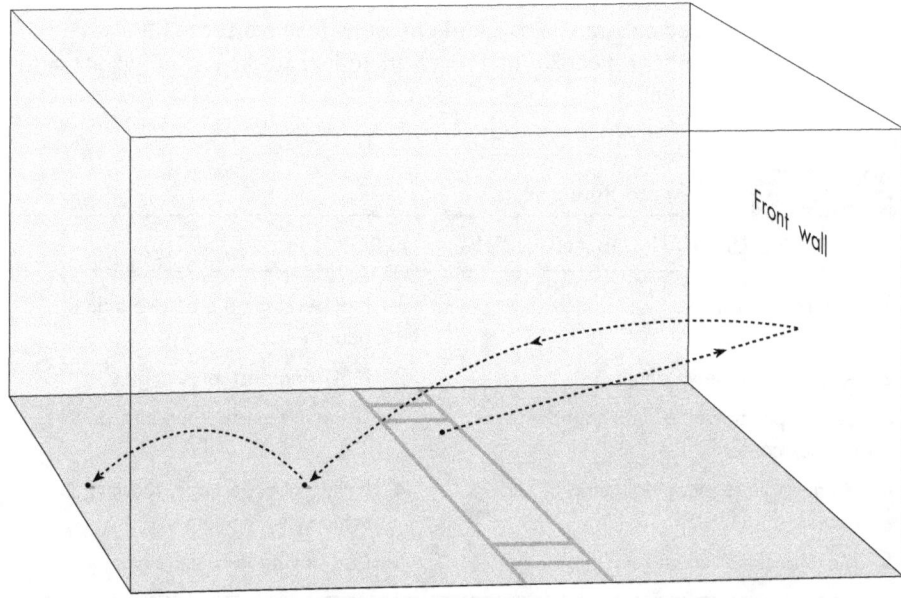

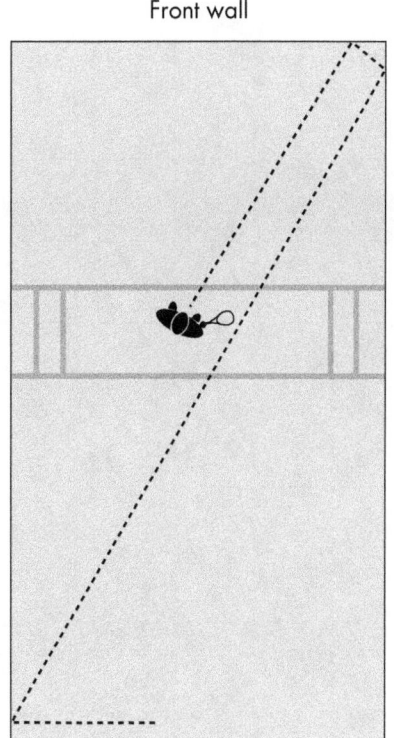

Figure 3.59 (on left) Overhead view of lob serve.

Figure 3.60 (on right) Overhead view of Z serve with midcourt setup.

Table 3.14 lists the fundamentals of the Z serve, as well as common errors.

High Z Serve

The **high Z** serve combines elements of both the lob serve and the Z serve to provide another excellent change-up serve. The ball will follow a crisscross path through the court, similar to the Z serve except for the last sidewall ricochet angle (see figure 3.61). The technique for hitting the shot is identical to the lob serve. The ball will be hit like a lob serve to a point high on the front wall and close to the

high Z

TABLE 3.14	Z Serve Summary
Z SERVE	**ERRORS**
1. Plan serve strategy.	1. Not developing pre-serve plan of attack.
2. Align close to same location each serve.	2. Serving predictably by alignment.
3. Begin with feet on short line.	3. Not using all of the service zone to build shot momentum.
4. Contact the ball low.	4. Contacting the ball too high.
5. Hit the ball low and flat.	5. Hitting the ball too high.
6. Hit at proper angle for deep back corner.	6. Hitting at wrong angle, leaving setup for strong offensive return.
7. Move to center court.	7. Not moving to center court.

Figure 3.61 (on left)
Overhead view of high Z serve.

Figure 3.62 (on right)
Drive serve drill box setup.

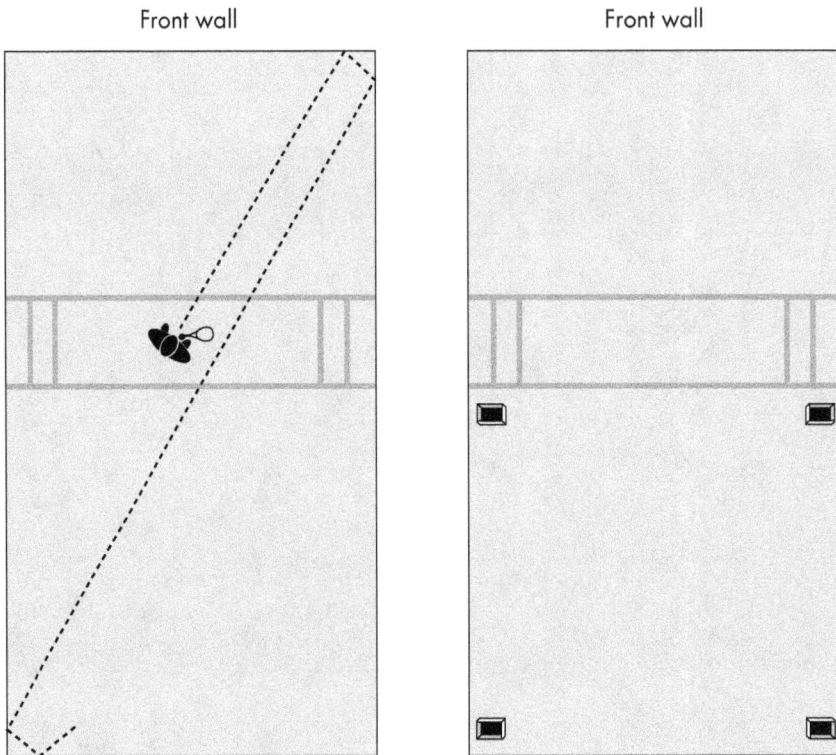

sidewall. The ball will rebound into the sidewall and drop to the floor behind the short line as it angles across the court toward the opposite sidewall. After hitting the floor, the ball will bounce high through center court and then drop to the floor again deep in the backhand corner, resulting in a difficult return. Move to center court position as soon as the ball passes the short line.

Serve Drills

Drive Serve Drill: Use drive serve techniques.

1. Place four boxes (1 foot by 2 foot opening) on their sides in the back corners and 2 to 3 feet behind the short line against the sidewalls (see figure 3.62). Equipment bags or other items of similar size may be substituted for the boxes.
2. Serve from the center of the service zone.
3. Drive serve to deep left (backhand) corner box. Observe where the ball hits the front wall and where it goes in relationship to the box.
4. Adjust the aiming point on the front wall to get the serve into the box, and repeat the serve. Observe and repeat until the proper aiming point is identified.
5. Place a marker on the spot on the front wall.
6. Repeat steps 2 through 5 for the other three box locations.
7. From the middle of the service zone, hit ten drive serves at each box by hitting to the appropriate front wall markers. Score a point for each time the ball hits the box.
8. A score of 4 or less for any one location means much more practice is needed. A score of 5 to 7 is adequate. Eight or more points indicates an advanced skill level on that serve.

Lob Serve Drill: (also use for Half-Lob and High Z Serve) Use appropriate lob serve techniques.

1. Mark two squares on the floor in each back corner as illustrated (see figure 3.63). Also, place two of the boxes (or other targets) from the drive serve drill in the back right and back left corners of the court.
2. Serve from the appropriate spot in the service zone for the type of lob serve being used in the drill.
3. Lob serve (crosscourt or down-the-wall) to the deep left (backhand) corner. Observe the angle and power needed to have the ball drop into the box in the corner. Adjust serve accordingly.
4. After a few warm-up serves (#3), hit ten lob serves (same type) to the deep left corner. Score five points for hitting the box, three points for hitting inside the 3-foot area, and two points for hitting inside the 5-foot area. One bonus point is awarded for hitting the sidewall behind the receiving line after bouncing on the floor. Fifty points are possible.
5. A score of 30 or more demonstrates consistency in the type of serve being executed, 20 to 29 is adequate, and under 20 indicates more practice is necessary.
6. Repeat #2 through #5, serving to the deep right-hand (forehand) corner.
7. Repeat entire drill sequence for the half-lob serve.
8. Repeat entire drill sequence for the high Z serve.

Figure 3.63
Lob serve drill setup.

Z Serve Drill: Use Z Serve techniques.

1. Place a marker on each sidewall, 5 feet from the back wall (see figure 3.64).
2. Serve from the center of the service zone.
3. Z serve to the back left (backhand) corner. Observe where the ball hits the front wall and where it goes in relationship to the back corner. Also, observe the possible Z effect coming off the sidewall at the end of the shot.
4. Adjust serve angles and the power of the shot to obtain the desired results (see figure 3.60).
5. After a few warm-up serves (#4), serve ten Z serves to the back left corner. Score one point for the path of the ball traveling crosscourt in a Z pattern to the left sidewall. Score two additional points if the ball hits the sidewall between the 5-foot marker and the back wall. Score one bonus point if the ball ricochets at the unusual Z angle off the sidewall at the end of the shot. Forty points are possible.
6. A score of 25 or more indicates consistency using the Z serve. A score of 15 to 24 is adequate. A score of 14 or less indicates more practice is necessary.

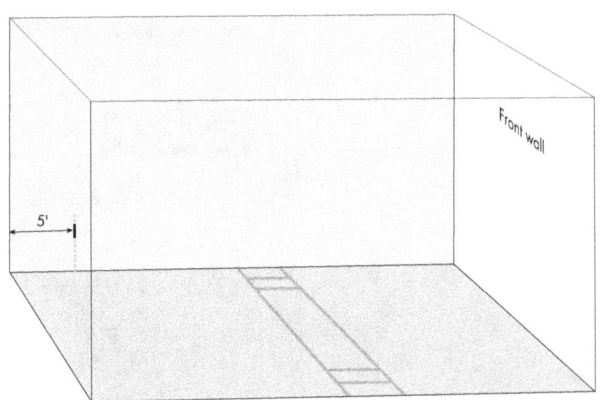

Figure 3.64
Z serve drill marker.

Return of Serve

If serve is the single most important aspect of the game of racquetball, then return of serve is the second most important. The more effective your opponent is at serv-

Figure 3.65
Alignment of receiver for return of serve.

ing, the higher skill you must have at returning serve. Because you can score points only when you are serving, you must be able to return the ball effectively and win rallies to earn the opportunity to serve.

Proper position is essential to effectively react to and return a variety of well-executed serves. The receiver should align in a position 5 to 6 feet in front of the back wall and close to the middle of the court (see figure 3.65). By adjusting this position 1 to 2 feet toward the backhand corner, a player can compensate for the crossover reach necessary when hitting a backhand return. Only minor variations of this starting point should be used, because a player with a good drive serve will be able to place his or her serve into the open corner resulting in a difficult return or an ace.

The objective for the return of serve should follow this order: (1) hit a kill shot return, (2) hit an aggressive passing shot, (3) hit a defensive shot, and (4) keep the ball alive any way possible. Whenever possible, hit a kill shot in an attempt to end the rally on the return of serve. If a kill shot is not feasible, go for an aggressive passing shot to also try to end the rally or force a weak return by the server. When the ball is above waist height, hit a defensive return to avoid a setup for the server to kill. There will be times when the only shot available is a desperation, keep-the-ball-alive-anyway-you-can return. In those instances, do whatever it takes to return the ball and give yourself a second chance in the rally.

Each serve is designed to create a different problem on the return of serve. Understanding these problems will help the receiver react and move into position to hit an effective return.

Table 3.15 lists the fundamentals involved in return of serve.

Dealing with Problems on Specific Serves

Drive Serve

1. React quickly.
2. Choose best return shot available.
3. Use back wall rebound whenever possible.
4. Avoid offensive setup on return.

Lob Serve, Half-Lob Serve, and High Z Serve

1. Read angle and power of shot.
2. Do not attack serve in front of receiving line, except after ball bounces.

TABLE 3.15 Return of Serve

1. Assume proper stance and position.
2. Observe server's alignment, stance, backswing, racket angle.
3. Observe ball angle off racket.
4. Backswing while quickly moving to contact point.
5. Use appropriate shot for return: kill shot, passing shot, defensive shot, keep-it-alive shot.

3. Be aware that contact point will usually force defensive return shot.
4. Avoid offensive setup on return.

Z Serve
1. Read angle and power of shot.
2. Anticipate sidewall contact point.
3. Determine type of return possible.
4. Avoid offensive setup on return.

Return of Serve/Serve Drill for Two Players

Play as a serving game.

1. To begin, one player will serve and the other will receive the serve.
2. The type of serve can be designated or random. The two participants should agree on one format before the drill begins.
3. Each server will receive five consecutive serving attempts. Fault and loss of serve rules apply for each attempt. (Two consecutive faults or one loss of serve shot equals one serving attempt.
4. The rally will last a maximum of four shots: the serve and three return shots. Score one point for the server on a serve that forces a poor offensive return or a defensive return. Score one point for the receiver on a return that does not allow a strong offensive return by the server. Score one point for the winner of any shot that ends the rally within the four-shot limit.
5. The first player to score fifteen points, win by one, is declared the winner of the drill game.

SKILL 6 — Advanced Offensive Shots

After you have learned the basic offensive shots discussed as "Skill 2," the kill shots and the passing shots, you are ready to be introduced to the advanced offensive shots that are commonly used by many experienced players. These advanced shots usually require greater accuracy and control than the basic offensive shots and can be very useful additions to any player's game. These shots include the **drop shot** (with a variation known as the soft corner kill), the splat, and the **overhead kill.**

drop shot
overhead kill

Drop Shot and Soft Corner Kill

The drop shot and soft corner kill are excellent change-ups during a drive shot rally. They can be particularly effective when a setup occurs in the frontcourt area. The drop shot is similar to a normal kill shot, with both using the same angles and trying to achieve a rapid second floor bounce on the rebound. The difference between a drop shot and a basic kill shot is a drop shot uses a controlled "pushing" motion with very little wrist action, rather than a full stroke with the racket. This causes the slower-moving ball to double bounce rapidly off the front wall when hit low and placed properly.

A soft corner kill is simply a drop shot hit into a front corner, using contact with the front wall and the sidewall (in either order) to cause the ball to lose its momentum and die faster than normal. The face of the racket must be angled accurately to place the ball low on the front wall or, in the case of a corner shot, into the corner

Figure 3.66

Splat shot to forehand corner.

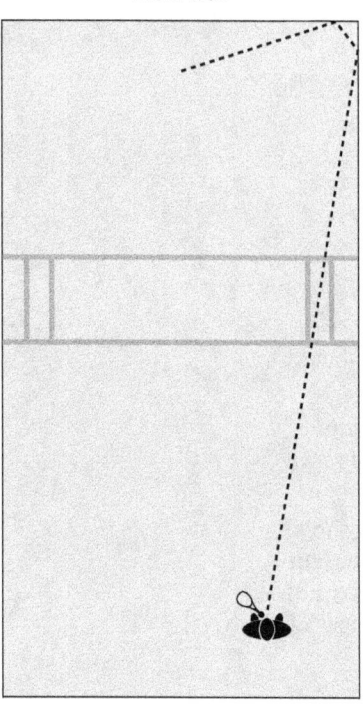

Figure 3.67

Position for drop shot drill.

area. The drop shot is usually hit from a frontcourt location and should be used only when your opponent is in the backcourt area.

A drop shot may occasionally be used from a position in the backcourt but requires even more finesse and skill to be accurate from this location. When your opponent is playing in the backcourt and is anticipating a drive shot or a ceiling shot, an accurate drop shot can be almost impossible to return.

Splat Shot

The splat shot should be used exclusively by more advanced players and requires great power and accuracy to be effective. The splat is hit from a position within 2 to 3 feet of a sidewall and is hit toward the front corner on the same side of the court with much power. The ball should be directed to hit the sidewall close to the front corner because this will put a great amount of spin on the ball as it rebounds into the front wall. This spin will cause the ball to "jump" off the front wall across the court almost parallel to the front wall. A player caught in backcourt has practically no chance to return the well-placed splat shot (see figure 3.66).

Overhead Kill Shot

The overhead kill shot is generally considered a low percentage shot by knowledgeable racquetball players. Advanced players seldom use it because any error in placement results in a setup for the opponent's return attempt. It is most frequently used by an impatient player trying to end a defensive ceiling ball rally in one stroke. The overhead kill shot should be used cautiously, but it may help to keep your opponents guessing, especially on defensive ceiling ball rallies, if they are aware that you have the shot in your repertoire.

The overhead kill shot is used almost exclusively from the backcourt area and is hit from a position above the head and slightly in front of the normal overhead contact point, using basic overhead stroke techniques. The racket face should direct the ball into one of the front corners, using the same angles and contact points as the corner kill or the pinch kill shots. This shot will usually be hit crosscourt into the forehand corner because most ceiling ball rallies take place deep in the backhand corner.

Advanced Offensive Shot Drills

Drop Shot Drill: Use forehand and backhand strokes.

1. Begin 1 to 2 feet in front of the service line and in the middle of the court (see figure 3.67).
2. Toss the ball off the front wall with the left hand to set up a drop shot attempt.
3. Return the tossed ball to the front wall with a drop shot or into one of the front corners with a soft corner kill shot.
4. Practice right and left corner shots, as well as front wall shots. Use both forehand and backhand strokes.

5. As you get more comfortable with the drop shots, move farther back into the court and toss, or lob hit, the ball for the setup. Repeat the drill frequently to become more consistent with your drop shots.
6. When a partner is available, have the partner hit the setup balls from a position deeper in the court and offset to one side (see figure 3.68).
7. Evaluate progress against past performance on drill.

Splat Shot Drill: Use forehand and backhand strokes.

1. Begin 6 to 8 feet in front of the back wall and 5 feet from the right sidewall, facing the right sidewall (see figure 3.69).
2. Drop the ball and hit a splat shot, using a forehand drive shot, to the right sidewall within a few feet of the right front corner.
3. Hit eight to ten practice shots from this position.
4. Move to the same relative position on the left side of the court, and face the left sidewall.
5. Repeat step #2 and #3 using a backhand stroke and hitting to the left front corner area.
6. Evaluate progress against past performance on drill.

Overhead Kill Shot Drill: Used primarily from backcourt area.

1. Begin in the center court area.
2. Drop the ball and hit a ceiling shot toward the backhand corner.
3. Move to the proper position and return the ceiling shot with an overhead kill attempt (see figure 3.70). Use either a corner kill shot or a pinch kill shot. Practice using each shot.

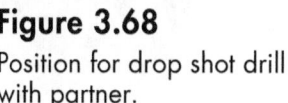

Figure 3.68
Position for drop shot drill with partner.

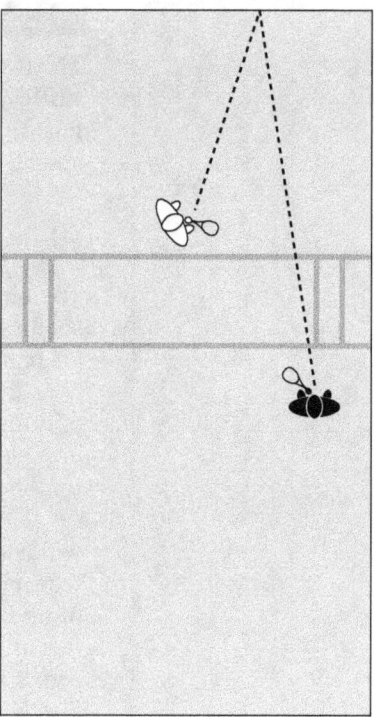

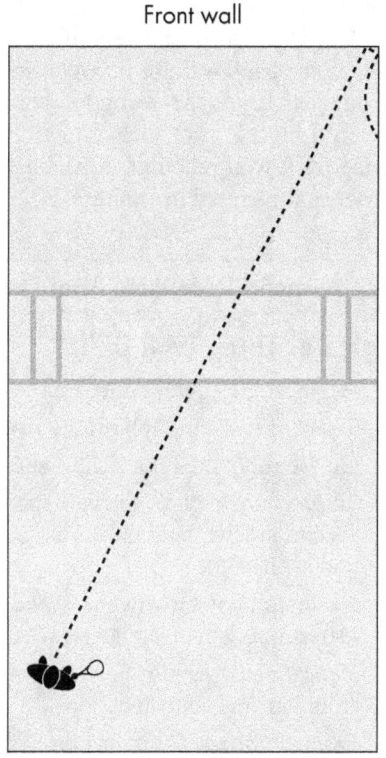

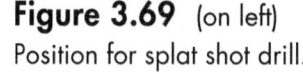

Figure 3.69 (on left)
Position for splat shot drill.

Figure 3.70 (on right)
Overhead kill drill.

4. Observe the results of your shot as the ball rebounds for the return shot. Evaluate the effectiveness of the overhead kill shot.
5. Evaluate progress against past performance on drill.

SKILL 7 — Advanced Defensive Shots

The two basic defensive shots discussed earlier in this section as "Skill 3" will be sufficient for most players when needing to make defensive shots or to sustain defensive rallies. For those who may want more, a defensive shot that is popular among the advanced players is the high Z or three-wall shot.

High Z or Three-Wall Shot

The object of any defensive shot is to keep a rally going when a good offensive shot is not possible and to not set up your opponent for a strong offensive shot of his or her own. The high Z, when hit properly, will accomplish both of these objectives. It can be hit with an overhead stroke for a high setup, as in a ceiling shot rally, or from anywhere on the court with a basic forehand or backhand stroke. The best place on the court to hit this shot is from the midcourt area because it allows for the angles that place the ball properly at the end of the shot.

The object of a high Z shot is to force a return shot from deep in the backcourt without giving your opponent opportunity for a strong offensive attempt. To be effective, the shot should be hit at a crosscourt angle, resulting in the desired Z path of the ball. The ball should be angled to hit high on the front wall and within 2 to 3 feet of the sidewall. The ball will ricochet into the sidewall and rebound diagonally across the court toward the back corner. The ball should pass over the center court area high enough to avoid a cutoff shot by your opponent. When hit with sufficient power, the ball will then Z off the sidewall (as in Z serve), drop to the floor, and bounce across the backcourt parallel to the back wall (see figure 3.71).

For the less powerful player, the high Z shot will follow a normal ricochet pattern and may even drop to the floor before reaching the second sidewall (see figure 3.72). This can also be a very effective shot if the angles result in the ball dropping close to the back wall, or into a back corner, on the second bounce. The ball should be directed to hit the second sidewall farther from the back wall than the more powerful high Z shot, thus allowing the ball to stay deep in the court without a strong back wall rebound. A backhand high Z shot should be hit to the crosscourt corner as illustrated in figure 3.73.

Advanced Defensive Shot Drills

High Z or Three-Wall Drill

1. Begin in the center court area.
2. Toss or hit a setup lob off the front wall for a forehand stroke (see figure 3.74).
3. On the rebound, hit a high Z shot to the left front corner.
4. Observe the path of the ball and the presence or absence of the Z effect off the second sidewall contact. Also observe where the second bounce occurs at the end of the shot.
5. Evaluate shot effectiveness and make adjustments on further shot attempts. Determine which shots you want to use.
6. Repeat steps #2 through #5 using backhand and overhead setups and hitting from various court locations.
7. Evaluate progress against past performance on the drill.

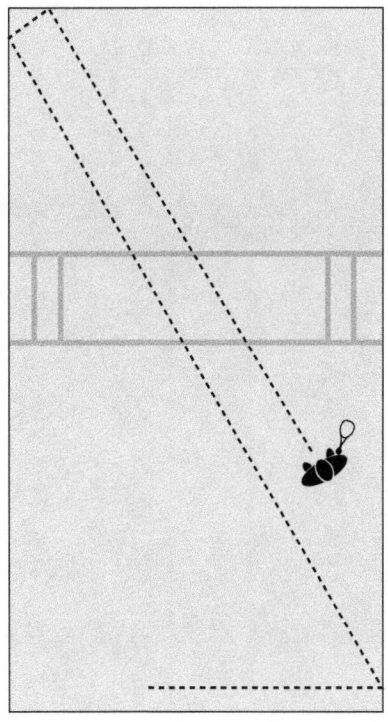
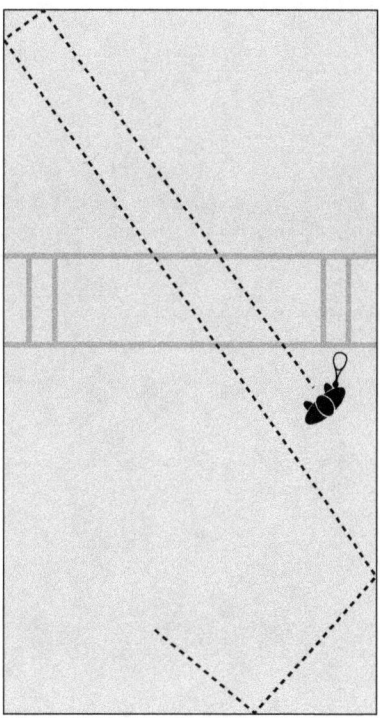

Figure 3.71 (on left) Powerful high Z shot with Z effect off sidewall.

Figure 3.72 (on right) Less powerful high Z shot with normal ricochet angles.

Figure 3.73 (on left) Backhand high Z shot angles.

Figure 3.74 (on right) High Z shot drill setup.

SECTION 4

Strategies

PSYCHOLOGICAL STRATEGIES FOR PERFORMANCE ENHANCEMENT

After a player has acquired the fundamentals of racquetball presented in Section 3, such as the forehand and backhand strokes, playing off the back wall, and the serve, it is time to learn the mental aspects of the game. Concentration during practice and competition is one key factor in improving and playing to one's own physical capabilities. The psychological learning tool of visualization is another excellent mental instrument that may enhance the execution of physical skills in racquetball. Finally, the management of stress and the development of relaxation skills, such as the pregame ability to relax and control anxiety, could be significant elements in improving performance.

Concentration

Concentration is the ability to focus one's attention on the task at hand, without allowing interference from outside distractions. In racquetball, players must learn to leave distractions off the court, or they will not be able to perform to their full capability. A player must concentrate on the current action on the court. Dwelling on previous actions, or thinking about outside items, can only detract from a player's ability to make the next shot correctly.

For beginning players, concentration may result in good footwork, proper body position, correct stroke technique, and other physical fundamentals that are involved in the learning process. For the more experienced players, the physical actions often become a matter of habit. For them, proper court position, good shot selection, anticipation of their opponent's next shot, and taking control of center court may result from good concentration during a game. Concentration on these factors can greatly enhance the on-court performance of any racquetball player.

Another important part of concentration in racquetball is to always watch the ball while it is in play. Losing sight of the ball during a rally can greatly decrease your chances of preparing for, and making, your next return shot attempt. Use your peripheral vision to know your opponent's court position, and focus your concentration on the ball location and its destination. The ball moves around the court so fast, and can change directions so quickly, that a lapse in concentration can easily result in losing the rally and the point or serve that goes with it. When attempting any stroke, you should watch the ball until after it has been hit by the racket. Too many players make the mistake of looking to see where the ball went before they hit it. When they do this, they frequently do not hit the shot properly because they have lost sight of the ball before the contact point.

Some players have the natural ability to turn off outside distractions, while others have difficulty doing the same thing. Learning to concentrate requires blocking outside interferences and continually reminding yourself to think about the immediate action on the court. Practice by doing this during play, and evaluate yourself after each rally and each match to determine the effectiveness of your concentration.

Visualization

Visualization, as it relates to racquetball, is imagining the performance of some racquetball skill or strategy in vivid detail. Maxwell Maltz reports in his book, *Psycho-Cybernetics,* that it has been proven beyond a doubt the human nervous system cannot tell the difference between a vividly imagined experience and an actual experience. (Have you ever awakened in a cold sweat from a stressful dream?) Synthesizing experiences with positive results in your mind can improve your ability to successfully perform those experiences in reality.

Many athletes have used visualization to improve their performance of specific skills in their sport. Golfers will step back and imagine the shot they are about to attempt, from addressing the ball to the follow-through at the end of the stroke. Then they will step up to the ball and repeat the performance that they rehearsed in their mind. In basketball, when preparing to shoot a foul shot, many players will mentally go through the shot before actually toeing the line and releasing the ball.

One study, reported in *Research Quarterly,* tested the basketball free throw shooting skills of three groups of students. They were all tested, then each group was given an assignment for the next 20 days. One group was to practice shooting free throws each day during the experiment. The second group was not to practice at all during that time. The third group engaged in visualization practice, mentally shooting free throws and correcting errors if they missed a shot in their mind. At the end of the study, the physical practice group improved 24 percent, the no practice group showed no change, and the mental practice group improved 23 percent. In this study, the results from mental practice were equal to the results from physical practice.

These visualization techniques can be used in racquetball to learn skills and strategies and to improve your playing ability. Take time to relax, and imagine yourself executing perfect technique on your strokes. Imagine yourself in game situations, hitting the perfectly placed kill or passing shot to end a rally. If you make a mistake, analyze it, correct the imagined flaw, and repeat the same situation perfectly in your mind. Concentrate intently on the experience. Vividly cover every detail. Repeat the most difficult shots or situations to strengthen your "memory" of the experience. This mental rehearsal will improve your ability to perform on the court.

Stress Management/Relaxation

The late Dr. Hans Selye, from the University of Montreal, was one of the first to scientifically study the problems of stress. In his book, *The Stress of Life,* his explanation of stress, transposed into simple terms, was the rate of wear and tear on the body in response to real or perceived demands placed upon it. Stress includes the self-induced tension or the pressure that we put upon ourselves when we are called upon to face challenges or problems. In sports competition, such as racquetball, this tension causes physiological reactions, including tightening of the muscles and shorter, quicker breathing patterns. Psychological reactions to stress include the inability to fully concentrate or focus on the task at hand and a lack of judgment regarding significance of actions or events. A player must learn to recognize and manage stress both before and during a match, using relaxation techniques to replace any negative influence this stress may have on his or her ability to play the game. Learn to control stress rather than allowing stress to control you.

Incorporating relaxation skills into preparation for competition can have a very positive effect on stress management and performance. Physical relaxation should be practiced daily, so the body will "learn" how to relax and relieve the muscle tension brought on by stress. Mental relaxation is a positive side effect of physical relaxation.

Preactivity Relaxation Technique

(This relaxation technique is a compilation of a variety of proven programs, including those presented by Dr. Maxwell Maltz in *Psycho-Cybernetics* and Allsen, Harrison, and Vance in *Fitness for Life: An Individualized Approach*.)

1. Place yourself in a warm, comfortable environment. Remove as much outside distraction as possible.
2. Lie down on a soft, comfortable surface, with your legs extended and your arms resting at your sides. (If this is not practical, a comfortable easy chair is an acceptable alternative.)
3. Take in a deep breath and hold. For 5 seconds, tighten every muscle in your body, including fingers and toes, neck and cheeks, and all major muscle groups.
4. At the end of 5 seconds, slowly exhale and try to allow your body to melt into the surface upon which you are lying (or sitting). Feel the tension leave your muscles as they relax and "flow" into the surface below.
5. Continue with slow, deep breathing, exhaling under control.
6. In your mind, picture a relaxing scene or pleasant memory from your past. Pay particular attention to details of that memory, such as the flowers or other beautiful scenery, the sounds that accompanied the experience, the warmth of the sun, the smell of fresh air or perfume, and any other incidental aspects that may make the memory more vivid. Let your mind wander and your body relax for at least 15 minutes each session.
7. Practice this technique daily until your body "learns" how to relax and remove tension and stress. Use these techniques before competition to remove outside pressure and to focus on the upcoming match.

During-Activity Relaxation Techniques

Learning to relax during competition is important to relieving stress and tension that may be detrimental to performance. There is neither time nor opportunity to use the same techniques listed for preactivity relaxation. Therefore, a different approach is necessary to accomplish relaxation during the match. Listed here are individual items that may be incorporated into a participant's thought process and actions to aid in relaxation during competition.

1. Have confidence in your own skills, game plan, and preparation. Know that you will play your best.
2. During a pause in the action, take in and slowly exhale a couple of deep breaths to relax tension.
3. Shake your arms and legs loosely and rotate your head in circles to relax these muscles.

4. Tighten the jaw and neck muscles and then relax them. This exercise has a relaxing effect on the rest of the body.
5. Use the 10-second time-out rule after a stressful rally or series of rallies to think and relax.
6. Call a full time-out to regroup and relax. Each player or team is allowed three 30-second time-outs in a game to fifteen and two 30-second time-outs in a game to eleven.

GAME STRATEGIES

The fundamentals that have been presented up to this point are all helpful in preparing to participate in a game of racquetball. The game strategies in this section will make a big difference in the effectiveness of these fundamentals when used in a game setting. The almost-perfect kill shot attempt is not effective if it is hit directly to an opponent standing in frontcourt. Your best serve could result in a side out if it is hit to your opponent's best return position. Learning when to hit certain shots, where to hit them, and how to make other decisions and adjustments during a game are all part of the strategy of racquetball.

Center Court Position

Whether center court position is considered as a skill or a strategy, it is such an important part of the game of racquetball that it should be covered in some detail. In a match between equally talented competitors, the player who controls center court will control the game. Therefore, learning where center court is located, and how to control center court, is a critical part of the game of racquetball.

Center court is not an exact spot on the court. It adjusts with the rally and covers the oval area of the court as illustrated in figure 4.1. The center point would be approximately 6 to 8 feet behind the short line and midway between the sidewalls. The speed of the rally, the power of the shots, and the shot selection of the participants will all determine adjustments made in center court positioning. Almost every ball that contacts a sidewall will pass through this center court area, giving you an opportunity to return most balls from here. Also, it is only a few steps to any area on the court to return your opponent's shot.

Controlling center court can be accomplished by using shot placement strategy. Learning to hit deep corner serves, ceiling shots, other defensive shots, and passing shots will keep your opponent moving out of the center court area and allow you to move in and "take control" of center court. Attempt to return to center court after every shot and force your opponent out of center court frequently, and you will find yourself in control of the game.

The Star Drill, explained in section 1, "Conditioning," emphasizes returning to center court. It is a good conditioning drill and teaches center court positioning. Use the Star Drill to reinforce the practice of returning to and controlling center court position.

Offense

There are two basic approaches to each shot in the game of racquetball: offensive or defensive strategy. Play an offensive shot when the situation gives you an opportunity to properly execute a rally-ending or difficult-to-return stroke. Play a defensive shot

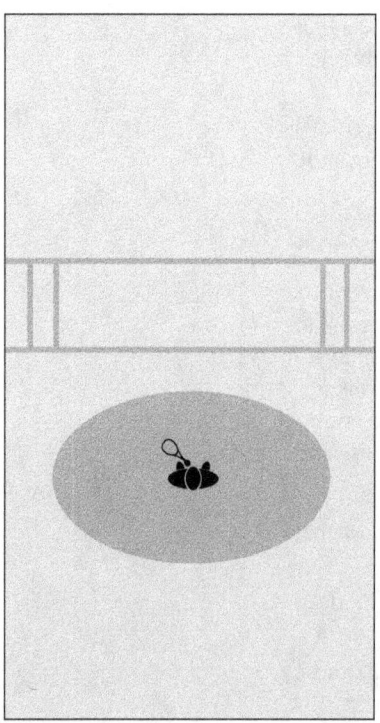

Figure 4.1
Center court position.

when you determine that a strong offensive shot is not the best decision because of game situation, lack of an offensive shot setup (hitting the ball from a low contact point), or some other factor. Knowing when to hit each style of return will produce strategic shot placements and more winning rallies.

Playing an offensive game of racquetball requires an aggressive attitude. Offensive shots are attacking shots and are designed to end rallies and score points. Drive serves, kill shots, and passing shots are examples of offensive weapons used in racquetball. Attacking your opponent's weaknesses, and using your strengths, are also part of playing an offensive game of racquetball.

Hitting defensive shots requires a player to be patient; the patient player knows that an opportunity may develop later in the rally to hit an aggressive winner. A player who can consistently hit sound defensive shots when necessary will often get a setup from an impatient or overaggressive opponent trying to end the rally with a poorly placed shot from a high ball contact point.

The Serve

The serve starts every rally, and an offensive or defensive serve will often dictate whether an offensive or defensive rally will ensue. Some items to consider before each serve are as follows: (1) What are your best serves, today and other days? (2) Which serve would cause the most difficult return for your opponent at this point in the game? (3) Does your opponent's alignment produce a weakness in his or her ability to return certain serves (too deep, too shallow, too far to one side)? (4) What do you need to do to properly execute the chosen serve? and (5) Are you prepared to move to center court following your serve, and then return the ball following your opponent's shot?

Every racquetball player has strengths and weaknesses in their game, and most players have one or more favorite serves in which they have developed confidence. Evaluate which serve(s) you are hitting more effectively during the early stages of a match, and use them frequently as competition continues.

During a match, you may find your opponent is having more difficulty hitting a strong return from a certain type of serve or a specific placement of serve. Use this information to continue to put pressure on your opponent's weakness. On the other hand, you may find that some serves result in a powerful return, such as a serve to the forehand side of the court. Discontinue using that serve and use only the more effective type and placement of serve for the remainder of the match. Also, be aware of an opponent who is becoming fatigued. Keep play moving along by minimizing rest time between serves to take advantage of your opponent's lack of conditioning for the match.

Before serving, always know where your opponent has lined up for the return of serve. Some players will move too far to one side of the court, or they will align too shallow or too deep for certain serves. Use their court position to your advantage by hitting a drive serve to the opposite side of the court if they offset too far, deep into the sidewall and corner if they are too shallow, or low drive serves that just pass the short line when they align too deep.

Before dropping the ball for the serve, know which serve you are going to use and what alignment and stroke adjustments are necessary to effectively execute your serve strategy. Do not try to decide what to do as you are dropping the ball or already swinging on the serve. Align in the appropriate location for each serve attempt, and try to not "telegraph" your strategy by your body position or stroke technique prior to striking the ball.

Prepare yourself to move back into center court after your serve passes the short line. Too many inexperienced players stand in the service zone and watch as their opponent hits passing shots to win the rally. You are almost always better prepared to play your opponent's return shot from center court. Defensive serves, such as the lob serve, are an excellent choice if you are having difficulty moving into center court position after your serve. Get there, and then get ready to move and hit your next shot.

The Rally

The continuous exchange of shots between the serve and the end of play is known as the rally. A rally where players are hitting powerful passing shots and attempting kill shots is referred to as an offensive rally. When players are using ceiling shots and around-the-wall balls to drive their opponents out of center court and back into the deep corners, it is called a defensive rally. A key point to remember is that during rallies between players of similar ability, the player who controls the center court area will more frequently be the winner.

The object of an offensive rally is to hit a shot that will end the rally. "Skill 2" in section 3 describes and illustrates the basic offensive shots: the passing shots and the kill shots. Whenever the ball is in a low position, enabling an attempt at one of these shots, a player should try to end the rally. Shot selection and placement are essential to success in an offensive rally. Keep the ball low. Hit the ball away from your opponent; make them cover as much court as possible. Know the rebound angles. Learn your opponent's strengths and weaknesses as the match develops. Take advantage of your opponent's weaknesses, while not playing into his or her strengths. One final key is to use your strengths as often as possible and to not try to win rallies by hitting shots that are your weaknesses because you will often set up your opponent for his or her rally-ending return. Be smart and be aggressive.

The object of a defensive rally is to hit shots that will keep the ball in play while forcing your opponent to move out of center court and deep to the corners for his or her return shots. "Skill 3" in section 3 describes and illustrates the basic defensive shots: the ceiling shot and the around-the-wall ball. Whenever possible, an offensive shot is recommended, but when the ball is too high for an accurate offensive stroke, a defensive shot should be used. The objective of a defensive rally is to allow you control of center court. Be patient and continue hitting defensive shots when the setup for your shot has a high contact point. Then when your opponent makes a poorly placed or weak return, hit an offensive winner.

In doubles, there is more concentration and strategy involved because of the number of players on the court. In order to hit a winner, you must know where both opponents are aligned, and place your offensive shots to defeat both players. You must also avoid hitting the ball into your partner. Defensive shots are frequently used in doubles rallies because there are not as many holes to attack with offensive shots. But remember to be aggressive and attack if you have an opportunity for an offensive shot.

Defense

The single most important factor in racquetball when your opponent is going to be hitting the ball is to be in the center court position. From here you will be able to cover most of the court effectively, using anticipation and proper footwork to move into position for your next shot. If you do not return to center court after your shot, a good opponent will simply hit his or her return where you have left a hole and will end the rally.

When returning serve, your alignment should be deep center court, 4 to 6 feet in front of the back wall. Read the server's stance and body language for clues to help you anticipate the serve and return. Then keep your eyes focused on the ball as it is dropped and struck on the serve, and move quickly to the court position necessary to make a proper return of the serve.

To play effective defense, it is also important to develop the ability to read your opponent's actions and anticipate shots before they actually occur. Observe body position, arm angles, racket location, and court position to give clues as to the upcoming shot selection and placement. A good player will always be aware of your court position, and you may be able to influence his or her decisions by feigning movement in one direction and then going the other way in anticipation of the shot placement.

Always keep your eyes on the ball and learn to anticipate its destination, not just its path. One of the most common errors of beginning players is lack of judgment in this area. Do not chase the ball around the court. Rather, observe and learn the rebound angles of the ball, which depend on its speed and the direction from which it is coming. This will allow more time for you to move into the proper position for your next shot.

In doubles, you should use the same basic principles as in singles, except that you will have a partner who can cover half of the court for you. Be aware of your partner's position, and work together to fill the holes and pick up any shots in your area of the court. Formations and alignments in doubles will be discussed further in the following section.

Alignments

Singles

In a game of singles, there are two specific alignments that should be used at various times during play: (1) the placement for the receiver on a serve and (2) center court position for each player after every shot (see figure 4.2).

The receiver of the serve should align at or close to the middle of the court and 4 to 6 feet in front of the back wall. This alignment allows for better court coverage

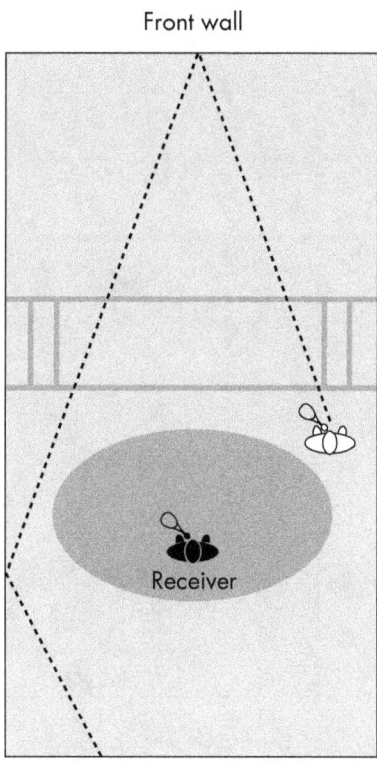

a   During serve

b   During rallies
receiver center-court position

Figure 4.2
Singles alignment.

in the areas where the serve will usually come, with enough depth to play the deep lob and other corner serves.

Center court position is important, as was explained earlier. From a center court alignment, a player can quickly move to almost any area of the court and have a chance to return most shots during a rally. When players do not return to center court after their shots, they leave an open area of the court for good opponents to attack with passing shots or other strategic shot placements.

Doubles

When two players on a team are on the court together, as in doubles, they must coordinate their alignments to effectively cover the court and assist one another. When serving or preparing to receive the serve, or during a rally (see figure 4.3), the doubles partners will have specific court areas to cover because of their alignment.

The team serving must have a player in one of the service boxes at the end of the service zone, while the other is hitting the serve from any legal serving location within the service zone (see figure 4.3a). After the ball passes the short line on the serve, they will move to either a side-by-side or an **I formation** (in doubles, when team members align with one in frontcourt and the other directly behind in backcourt; see figure 4.3b), and play the rally from there. Some teams choose to divide the court diagonally and play with **front/back** responsibilities (see figure 4.3c).

I formation

front/back

Figure 4.3
Doubles alignment.

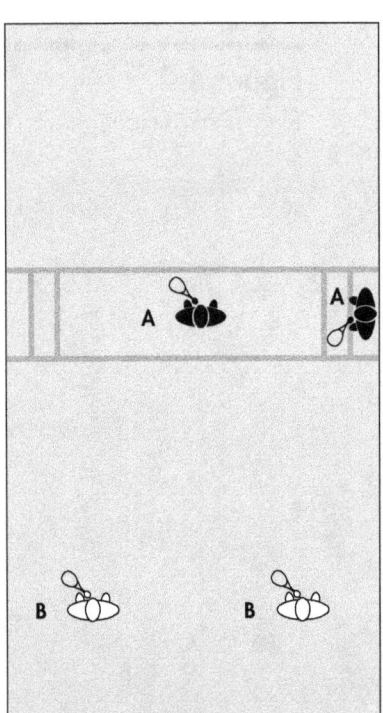

a During serve
   Team A—serving
   Team B—receiving

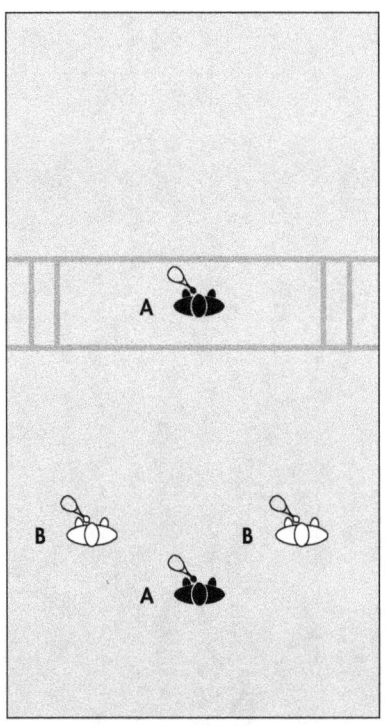

b During rallies
   Team A—I formation
   Team B—side-by-side formation

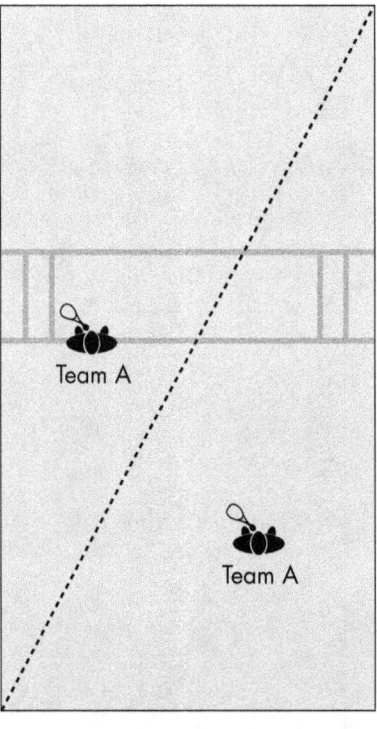

c During rallies
   diagonal front/back formation

The team receiving serve will begin in a side-by-side alignment (see figure 4.3a). After returning the serve, they may stay in that alignment as they move to control center court, or they may adjust to an I or diagonal formation for the remainder of the rally.

In cutthroat, the server will align, serve, and cover the court as if in a game of singles. The two receivers align and work together as a doubles team to receive the serve and play the rally. The server must use doubles strategy on shot selection and placement because he or she is playing against a doubles team (two players). The two receivers must use singles strategy because they are playing against only one opponent.

Anticipating Opponent's Strategies

Anticipation is a key factor in many aspects of a racquetball match. You must learn to anticipate your opponent's serve and rally strategy on shot selection, shot placement, court movement, and positioning. Racquetball is such a fast-paced, split-second game that any advantage you can gain through anticipation may be the difference between making or missing your next shot. Understanding your opponent's psychological strategy is also important.

Serve

When trying to anticipate your opponent's strategy, there are a number of factors to observe as he or she prepares to serve the ball. These include alignment, body position, racket face angles, eye contact, and other items that may give "clues" as you try to anticipate the serve. At the beginning of the stroke, is there a directional clue given by the foot placement, the downswing, or the body angle? Is he or she stepping to one side or the other to guide the ball? Did the server give any other clues where the ball would be going? What has he or she been hitting that has been successful against you, and does it look like the same shot is coming at you again? Learning to observe and evaluate these possible clues could help you anticipate the serve, allowing you more opportunity to make a strong return.

Rally

During the rally, anticipating your opponent's strategy is critical to being able to consistently make your return shots. If you rely strictly on reaction, you will find yourself waving at the ball as it passes you and dies in a distant corner of the court. A good player learns to gather clues from his or her opponent and to recall the previous strategies used during the match. This information is gathered and analyzed to assist in anticipating the next shot by the opponent.

Many pieces of information can be gathered to support your anticipation efforts during the rally. Items such as your opponent's court location, body position, type of swing, racket face angle, contact point, and follow-through are some of the clues available. Remembering what shots your opponent has attempted, and which were successful, will also result in better anticipation.

A good opponent will be observing your court location and will play the ball away from your position whenever possible. He or she will also make an effort to play away from your strengths and to your weaknesses. Pay close attention during the match to where your opponent is attacking you and from where you may be hitting your weaker shots. Use this information to be better prepared to play these shots as the match progresses.

Psychological Strategy

Many players will try to use "mind games" on you to gain an advantage during a match. If you listen to them, and believe what they are saying, or allow them to impress you with some form of psychology other than words, you become their victim. Be aware of the following tactics and do not let them disturb you during competition: the Flatterer, the Complainer, the Jabberer, the Intimidator, and the Irritator.

The Flatterer will try to tell you how good you are and will constantly be telling you what *great* shots you are making or what a *great* attempt you made on a missed shot. He or she is trying to convince you to be impressed with yourself and to become overconfident. Just remember that you are only as good as your next shot in a competitive game of racquetball.

The Complainer will have something to complain about on every play. "The ball must be wet," "The floor is dusty," or "I didn't get enough time to warm up properly" are examples of a complainer's logic. You must ignore these complaints, knowing they are meant to create a negative atmosphere on the court and are designed to take your concentration away from the game itself.

The Jabberer is constantly talking to himself or herself about something. It will usually be a combination of self-criticism, complaints about how lucky your shots are, and self-instruction. He or she may mumble such things as "Quit hitting the ball right to him, you idiot," "I can't believe she could make that shot one out of a hundred tries," or "Keep the ball down, *down!*" If you listen to the constant chatter coming from the Jabberer, you will be distracted from the concentration that must go into your competition.

The Intimidator will try to overwhelm you with his or her court presence and powerful shots, especially during warm-ups and at the beginning of the match. Booming forehands, loud, echoing shouts, and the unspoken "Walk around me; I am not moving out of your way" are meant to create an atmosphere of intimidation on the court. He or she is saying, "Don't get in my way, or in the way of my shot, if you know what is good for you." Once the initial efforts of the Intimidator are ignored, he or she will usually return to a normal player attempting to play the way racquetball is supposed to be played. Smile, and even chuckle a little, when you meet up with an Intimidator, and force him or her to "put up or shut up" during play.

The Irritator is a combination of all of the above, and more. It is the intent of Irritators to bother you any way they can, to break your concentration, and to gain a psychological advantage over you. They will show up late for the match, take too long to warm up, and then stall at the most inopportune times during play to create dissention on the court. Do not let them bother you. You can let them know how you feel about flagrant violations of courtesy and good sportsmanship, but always keep a smile on your face and laugh about it. In fact, you may become the irritation if they think they have failed to get to you!

Adjusting to Characteristics of Your Opponent

There are so many variables that make up a good racquetball player that no single characteristic should be overwhelming in an opponent. Attributes such as size, speed, power, and aggressiveness should all be considered while determining your match strategy. A player must be able to adjust to these characteristics and can do so only when he or she understands the advantages, and weaknesses, of each.

Size

The very large player (tall or wide) can be an intimidating figure in the confines of a racquetball court. He or she may also have an advantage of long arms (long reach) and an ability to produce great power in his or her shots. The disadvantage of being large is usually in the speed and quickness area and, possibly, in conditioning level. Do not allow a larger player's presence to intimidate you. Know your strengths and use them against his or her weaknesses. Keep the ball in play and move your shots around the court to test your opponent's quickness and endurance. Hit shots that will force him or her to move from front to back and side to side. Determine if your opponent can hit solid forehand and backhand shots, and place your returns to take advantage of his or her weakest areas.

Speed

An opponent with speed poses problems in finding holes for your shots. Quick players have the advantage of being able to retrieve many shots slower players could not retrieve. There are no apparent weaknesses associated directly with speed, so you must evaluate deeper and find other areas of your opponent's game that can be attacked. Playing fast-paced, hard-hitting rallies allows these players to use their strengths against you. One strategy might be to slow the game down with defensive shots, such as the ceiling shot or around-the-wall ball. Test their patience with a controlled-tempo rally. Be patient and wait for an offensive opportunity to develop, then end the rally with your best kill shot.

Power

A power player is one who tries to "blow you off the court" with explosive shots from anywhere on the court. One advantage of a power player is that he or she can hit shots that will pass you before you are able to react to the ball. One of the primary disadvantages facing a power player is that many of his or her shots will rebound off the back wall, allowing you a second chance for a return shot. Keep the ball high and deep in the court, not allowing a low contact point for your opponent's power shots. Then, when an opportunity presents itself, hit a kill shot or a passing shot to end the rally.

Aggressiveness

Playing against a very aggressive opponent can be either a frustrating or a rewarding experience, depending on your strategic approach to the rallies. The advantage for an aggressive player is that he or she is always attacking and always keeping pressure on the opponent by the fast pace of his or her rallies. The disadvantage is that aggressive players often have the tendency to be impatient. They will go after everything, often cutting off shots heading for back wall rebounds and hitting the ball from undesirable contact points. Slow the rally down by hitting some high-Z shots, around-the-wall balls, or ceiling shots. Then capitalize when the aggressive player makes a mistake, and hit a winner to end the rally.

Learning by Watching

As a closing comment, the author recommends as much exposure to racquetball as your time will allow by playing, practicing, studying, and observing the game. Play and practice as much as your allotted court time and energy will permit. Study the rules and any other information, especially on skills and strategy, that will enhance your understanding of the game. Watch others play, not just as a spectator, but as a student of the action on the court. Analyze their shot selection, their placements, their court positioning. Critique (to yourself) the results of their strategy, and try to determine why it did, or didn't, work for them. Decide what might have been a better approach to a situation, and speculate what you would have done differently for a more effective result. Learn from the play (good and bad) of others.

You will find that as you learn and understand more about racquetball, you will achieve great personal satisfaction by executing your skills and strategy on the court. Whether for recreation, exercise, or intense competition, racquetball will be an exciting and rewarding activity you can participate in for the rest of your life.

References

Allsen, P.E., J.M. Harrison, and B. Vance. 1993. *Fitness for life: An individualized approach*. Madison, WI: Brown & Benchmark.

Clark, L.V. 1960. Effects of mental practice on the development of a certain motor skill. *Research Quarterly* 31: 560.

Maltz, M. 1972. *Psycho-cybernetics*. No. Hollywood, CA: Wilshire.

Selye, H. 1978. *The stress of life*. New York: McGraw-Hill.

Glossary

SECTION 5

AARA American Amateur Racquetball Association; now replaced by the USRA

ace A legal serve that the receiver does not touch

anticipation Predicting what will happen next on the court

around-the-wall ball A defensive shot that hits three walls (a sidewall, the front wall, and the opposite sidewall) before touching the floor

avoidable hinder Interference with an opponent that results in a point or a side out, including failure to move, stroke interference, blocking, moving into the ball, pushing, intentional distractions, view obstructions, and wetting the ball

backcourt The area from the receiving line to the back wall; the last approximate one-third of the court

backhand A stroke hit on the opposite side of the body from the racket hand

backswing The act of taking the racket back in preparation for hitting the ball

back wall The rear wall of the court

ceiling fault A serve that strikes the ceiling after hitting the front wall

ceiling shot A defensive shot that hits the ceiling first then hits the front wall, drops to the floor, and bounces deep into the backcourt area

center court The oval-shaped area on the court whose middle is 6 to 8 feet behind the short line and equal distance from the side walls

contact point The spot during the stroke where the racket strikes the ball

continental grip Hand placement on the racket handle between the handshake forehand and backhand positions

court hinder When the ball strikes an obstruction on the court, such as the door handle, a light fixture, or a ball can. The play is stopped and the point is replayed

crotch A point on the court where two surfaces meet, such as a wall and the floor or two walls

cutthroat A racquetball game with three players; the server plays against the other two players

dead ball Any ball that is no longer in play

dead-ball hinder Any hinder that results in the serve being replayed; a hinder with no points or side outs

defensive shot Any shot designed to maneuver the opponent out of center court position and to extend the rally

dehydration A physical condition brought on by an excessive loss of body fluids without adequate replacement

die A ball loses momentum and bounces a second time to end a rally

doubles A racquetball game with four players, two on each team

down-the-wall pass When the ball rebounds off the front wall, parallel and close to a sidewall, and travels into the backcourt area. Also called a wallpaper pass

drive serve A powerful serve that travels in a relatively straight line off the front wall

drive serve fault When the server violates the drive serve zone during the serve

drive serve zone The area 36 inches from each sidewall in the service zone

drive shot A powerful shot that travels in a straight, flat line

drop shot A soft shot that is hit with deception to rebound off the front wall and die quickly

Eastern forehand The most common racquetball grip, also called the "handshake" grip

fault serve An illegal serve that must be replayed. Two consecutive fault serves result in the loss of serve

follow-through The completion of the stroke action after contacting the ball with the racket

foot fault An illegal serve where the server's foot lands completely outside the service zone; in doubles, the server's partner being out of the service box during the serve

forehand A stroke hit on the same side of the body as the racket hand

front/back Similar to the I formation in doubles, with the court divided diagonally

frontcourt The area of the court in front of the service line

garbage serve A half-lob serve that bounces to shoulder height on the receiver as it travels deep into a back corner of the court

half-lob serve A short lob serve hit to the front wall about head high and bouncing to shoulder height on the receiver while traveling into the back corner of the court

handout In doubles, the loss of serve by the first server of the doubles team

high Z A ball hit high to the front wall that rebounds into the near sidewall and crosscourt to the opposite sidewall. A legal high Z serve must hit the floor before hitting the opposite sidewall

hinder Interference with the flow of play; includes dead ball hinders, point hinders, safety hinders, and court hinders

I formation In doubles, when team members align with one in frontcourt and the other directly behind in backcourt

kill shot A ball hit so low on the front wall that it quickly bounces twice on the floor, making it impossible, or nearly impossible, to return

lob A ball hit high and soft to the front wall, rebounding and bouncing with a high arc into the backcourt

long fault A serve that strikes the back wall before bouncing on the floor

match In racquetball, winning two games out of three

midcourt The area of the court between the service line and the receiving line

offensive shot An aggressive shot attempting to win the rally

out of order serve In doubles, when a team member serves out of order, resulting in a loss of serve and a handout

out serve loss of serve

overhead kill A kill shot using an overhead stroke

overhead smash grip The proper grip used when contacting the ball above shoulder height, also called the Western grip

overhead stroke The stroke used to hit the ball when the contact point is above the shoulder

passing shot A shot that rebounds past the receiver and into the backcourt

point hinder A hinder resulting in a point or a loss of serve

protective eyewear Safety glasses required by rule to be worn when entering a racquetball court

racket face The stringed area of the racket

racket head The stringed hitting surface of the racket

rally The continuous series of hits following the serve until the point is over

ready position The ideal body position a player assumes prior to hitting any stroke except the serve

receiver The player waiting to receive the serve

receiving line Court marking line for service 5 feet behind the short line

rollout A perfect kill shot where the ball strikes so low on the wall that it doesn't bounce, but rolls out on the floor and is impossible to return

safety hinder When a player stops play to avoid contact with another player that may cause an injury

safety zone The court area between the short line and the receiving line

screen Interfering with the opponent's view of the ball; on the serve it is a fault

serve Putting the ball in play to start each rally

service line The line on the floor closest to the front wall

service zone The area between the outer edges of the service line and the short line

short fault A serve hitting the floor before passing the short line

short line The back line of the service zone

shot placement The spot or direction where the shot is meant to be hit

side out The loss of serve, and serve goes to the opponent

singles A racquetball game with two players playing against each other

thong The safety cord attached to the end of the racket handle and the player's wrist; used to prevent the racket from leaving the hand and causing a safety hazard during play

three-wall fault A serve that strikes three walls before hitting the floor

USRA United States Racquetball Association

wallpaper pass See "down-the-wall pass"

Western grip Grip used when contacting the ball above the shoulder, also called the overhead smash grip

Z serve A serve where the ball is hit toward the front wall, rebounds into a sidewall, bounces on the floor as it goes crosscourt, and then strikes the opposite sidewall deep in the court

Index

American Amateur Racquetball
    Association (AARA), 1, 2
American Collegiate Racquetball
    Association (ACRA), 1, 2
Anticipation, 13
Avoidable hinders, 16

Backhand, 8, 21–23, 30
Backhand grip, 21, 23
Backhand stroke, 30–34
    drills, 34–36
    errors related to, 33
    fundamentals, 32
Backswing, 16, 25–26, 29, 30
Back wall, 5
Back wall shots, 59–69
    back wall rebound from a corner,
        61–62, 63, 66
    back wall rebound on the fly,
        60–61, 64, 66
    desperation back wall shots,
        67–69
    drills, 64–67
    summary table, 64

Ceiling fault, 14
Ceiling shots, 54–58
    crosscourt ceiling shot, 55, 58–59
    down-the-wall ceiling shot, 55, 57
Center court, 4
Concentration, 87–88
Contact point, 21
Continental grip, 22–23, 99
Corner kill, 49–50, 52–53
Court, specifications for, 16–17

Court hinder, 16, 99
Crosscourt pass, 43, 44
Crosscourt sidewall pass, 42, 43, 44
Crotch serve, 15
Cutthroat, 14, 95, 99

Dampeners, 11
Dead ball, 18
Dead ball hinders, 16, 99
Defensive shots, 53–59
    advanced, 84–85
    around-the-wall ball, 53, 56
    ceiling shots, 54–58
    drills, 57–58
    errors related to, 56
    high Z (three-wall shot), 84
Desperation back wall shots, 67–69
Die, 41
Doubles, 14, 94
Down-the-wall ceiling shot, 55, 57
Down-the-wall pass, 42–43, 46
Drive serve, 14, 71–73, 78
    drills, 78
Drive serve fault, 14
Drive serve zone, 14
Drop shot, 81–83

Eastern forehand, 19
Equipment, 9–12
    accessories, 12
    bag, 12
    clothing, 9
    dampeners, 11
    footwear, 2, 9
    protective eyewear, 6, 9

    rackets, 9–12
    racquetballs, 12
Etiquette, guidelines for, 17–18

Fault serve, 14
Follow-through, 16, 28–29
Foot fault, 14, 70
Forehand, 8, 19–21, 25–29
Forehand grip, 19–21
Forehand stroke, 25–29
    drills, 34–36
    errors related to, 33
    fundamentals, 29
Frontcourt, 42–43
Front wall kill, 48–50

Gallery, 15
Game strategies, 87–98
    alignments, 93–94
    anticipating opponent's
        strategies, 95–96
    center court position, 90
    characteristics of opponent,
        adjusting to, 96–97
    defense, 92–93
    offense, 90–92
    opponent, 96–97
Garbage serve, 75
Gloves, 12
Grip, 19–24
    backhand grip, 21–22
    common grip errors, 23
    continental grip, 22
    Eastern forehand, 19–20
    forehand grip, 19–21

overhead smash, 22–23
  Western grip, 22–23

Half-lob serve, 75, 76, 79, 80
Handout, 15
Handshake grip, 19–20
High Z serve, 77, 78, 79, 80
High Z shot, 84
Hinders, types of, 16

I formation, 94

Killshot, 3
Kill shots, 46–53
  corner kill shot, 49–50
  drills, 52–53
  errors related to, 52
  front wall kill shot, 48–49, 52
  overhead kill shot, 83–84
  pinch kill shot, 50–51
  soft corner kill, 81–82

Learn Your Lessons, 3
Line drill, 5
Lob, 68, 74–75, 77, 80
Lob serve, 74–75, 77, 80
Long fault, 14

Match, 3, 17
Midcourt, 64

Offensive shots, 41–53
  advanced, 81–84
  drills, 45–46, 52–53
  drop shot, 81–82
  kill shots, 46–53, 81–82
  passing shots, 41–46
  splat shot, 82
Out of order serve, 15
Out serve, 14
Overhead kill shot, 82, 83–84
Overhead smash grip, 22–23
Overhead stroke, 36–41
  drills, 40–41
  errors related to, 40
  movements in, 37–39

Passing shots, 41–46
  crosscourt pass, 43
  crosscourt sidewall pass, 43–45
  down-the-wall pass, 42–43

drills, 45–46
  errors related to, 45
Pinch kill shot, 50–51, 53
Playing Smart, 3
Point hinders, 16
Protective eyewear, 6, 9
Psychological factors, 87–90
  concentration, 87–88
  stress management, 88–89
  visualization, 87–88

Racket covers, 12
Racket face, 15
Racket head, 26
Rackets, 1–2, 9–12
Racquetball (*see also* Skills):
  conditioning for, 3–8
  court, 16–17
  equipment, 9–12
  etiquette, 17–18
  game action, 14–15
  history of, 1–2
  organizations for, 1–2
  participants, number of, 14
  physical skills for, 13
  publications and resource materials, 2–3
  rules of game, 14–16
  safety guidelines, 6, 9
  scoring, 17
Racquetball Magazine, 3
Racquetballs, 12
Racquetball skills, *see* Skills
Ready position, 24
Receiver, 14
Receiving line, 15
Return of serve, 15–16, 70, 79–81
  drills, 81
  guidelines for, 15–16
Return of serve and rally, rules of, 15–16

Safety hinder, 16
Safety zone rules, 14
Scoring, rules of, 17
Screen, 14
Serve, 70–81
  drills, 78–79
  drive serve, 71–73, 78–80, 91
  errors related to, 73, 75, 77
  half-lob serve, 75–76

high Z serve, 77–78
  lob serve, 74–75
  return of serve, 15–16, 79–81
  rules of, 15–16
  Z serve, 76–78
Serve-and-rally action, 3
Service line, 5, 16
Service zone, 14–16
Serving, rules of, 14–16
Shoes, 9
Short fault, 14
Short line, 5, 14
Shot placement, 13
Side out, 15
Singles, 14, 93–94
Skills:
  back wall shots, 59–69
  defensive shots, 53–59
  grip, 19–24
  offensive shots, 41–53
  ready position, 24
  serve, 70–81
  stroke, 25–41
  wrist action, 19–20, 24
Soft corner kill, 81–82
Star drill, 4
Stress management, 88–89
Stretching, warm-up, 7–8
Stroke:
  backhand stroke, 30–34
  forehand stroke, 25–29
  overhead stroke, 36–41

Three-wall fault, 14
Total Racquetball, 3

United States Racquetball Association, 1, 2

Visualization, 87–88

Wallpaper pass, 42–43
Warm-up:
  basic guidelines, 7
  stretches for, 7–8
Western grip, 22–23
Wide-angle pass, 43
Wrist action, 19–20, 24

Z serve, 71, 76–78

For Product Safety Concerns and Information please contact our EU representative GPSR@taylorandfrancis.com
Taylor & Francis Verlag GmbH, Kaufingerstraße 24, 80331 München, Germany

www.ingramcontent.com/pod-product-compliance
Lightning Source LLC
Chambersburg PA
CBHW081422230426
43668CB00016B/2325